Atlas of Brainy Challenges

Map It!™

★

From America's #1 Road Atlas

Volume 1

⊕ RAND M^{c}NALLY

Map It!™

Concept and Editorial Direction: Joan Sharp, V.P. Publishing
Cover Design: Erika Nygaard
Interior Design: Erika Nygaard
Writer: Mary Bunker
Design Production: Erika Nygaard
Puzzle Tester: Jacqueline Henkel
Product Management Director: Jenny Thornton
Production: Carey Seren
Cartography: Gregory P. Babiak, Robert Ferry, Justin Griffin, Steve Wiertz, Thomas F. Vitacco

Published in U.S.A.
Printed in Canada
June 2017
PO# 55949
ISBN 0-528-01824-8

If you have any questions, concerns or even a compliment, please visit us at randmcnally.com/contact or e-mail us at: consumeraffairs@randmcnally.com or write to:
Rand McNally
Consumer Affairs
P.O. Box 7600
Chicago, Illinois 60680-9915

randmcnally.com

Rand McNally *CarTainment*

Maps keep adventure alive.

Think about it. When you look at a map you always see something you didn't see before. That's an invitation to explore!

And we're not just saying that because we're Rand McNally and because we've been guiding travelers and the geographically curious with our maps and atlases for more than 100 years. We say it because it's true.

Maps captivate. Maps are a remarkable mix of colorful artistry and scientific precision. Maps inspire us to discover new adventures and steady us in moments of disorientation. They fill us with wanderlust and enrich life's journey.

Find your next adventure using this atlas of seek & find map challenges. We'll re-introduce you to those places you've been or open your eyes to some you never knew existed. Get lost in the depth of our beautiful cartography while searching all corners of the map for places familiar or places waiting to be discovered.

Contents

Map Legend

Roads and related symbols

Limited-access, multilane highway—free; toll

New road (under construction as of press time)

Other multilane highway

Principal highway

Other through highway

Other road (conditions vary — local inquiry suggested)

Unpaved road (conditions vary — local inquiry suggested)

Ramp; one way route

Car ferry (with toll unless otherwise indicated on map)

Tunnel; mountain pass

Railroad; Intracoastal Waterway

Interstate highway; Interstate highway business route

U.S. highway; U.S. highway business route

Trans-Canada highway; Autoroute

Mexican highway or Central American highway

State/provincial highway; secondary state/provincial, or county highway

Great River Road; Great Lakes Circle Tour

Lewis & Clark Trail Highway; Lincoln Highway; Historic Route 66

Scenic route

Service area; toll booth or fee booth

Interchanges and exit numbers
For most states, the mileage between interchanges may be determined by subtracting one number from the other.

Highway distances (segments of one mile or less not shown):
Cumulative miles (red): the distance between arrows
Cumulative kilometers (blue): the distance between arrows
Intermediate miles (black): the distance between intersections & places

Comparative distance
1 mile = 1.609 kilometers   1 kilometer = 0.621 mile

Cities & towns size of type on map indicates relative population

National capital; state or provincial capital

County seat or independent city

City, town, or recognized place—incorporated; unincorporated

Urbanized area

Separate cities within metropolitan area

Parks, recreation areas, & other points of interest

National park

Other national park system location

National forest, national grassland, or city park; Wilderness area

State/provincial park system location; State/provincial forest

State/provincial park system location—with campsites; without campsites

Campsite; wayside or roadside park

Point of interest, historic site or monument

Airport

Building

Foot trail

Golf course or country club; ski area

Hospital or medical center

Military or governmental installation; military airport

Native American tribal lands

Ranger station

Rest area—with toilets; without toilets

Tourist information center; port of entry

Physical features

Mountain peak; highest point in state/province

Lake; intermittent lake; dry lake

River; intermittent river

Dam; swamp or mangrove swamp

Desert; glacier

Continental divide

Other symbols

Area shown in greater detail on inset map

Inset map page indicator (if not on same page)

County or parish boundary and name

State or provincial boundary

National boundary

Time zone boundary

Latitude; longitude

Map abbreviations

Listed below are some of the commonly used abbreviations on our maps. For a complete list of abbreviations that appear on the maps, go to www.randmcnally.com/ABBR.

Bfld.	Battlefield	N.P.	National Park
Cr.	Creek	N.R.A.	National Recreation Area
I.	Island	N.W.R.	National Wildlife Refuge
Int'l	International	S.H.S.	State Historic Site
L.	Lake	S.N.A.	State Natural Area
N.H.P.	National Historic Park	S.P.	State Park
N.H.S.	National Historic Site	S.R.A.	State Recreation Area
N.M.	National Monument	W.M.A.	Wildlife Management Area

Let's get mapping!

The Rand McNally *Map It!*™ *Atlas of Brainy Challenges* puts your navigation skills to the test with 24 seek & find puzzles. Each puzzle uses a section of a state map from America's #1 Road Atlas.

Have fun ticking off the creatively cultivated and uniquely categorized puzzle challenges comprised of cities, towns and counties; lakes, ponds and rivers; parks and campgrounds—all unique to the state. Chances are you'll never look at a map the same way again!

How to *Map It!*™

Choose the state you'd like to explore, check out the puzzle challenges selected for each category listed, grab a pencil or highlighter, and get started. Once you seek a challenge on the map, *Map It!*™ with a circle or highlight, then jot down the coordinates next to the listing on the left hand page to mark the challenge as solved. Coordinates can be found using the letter and number grids that frame each map (we call this grid a "bingo.") For example, if a town named *Fallsville* is on the list, it may be found in the coordinates A2, (as shown to the right.)

Helpful Tips

- Use the legend on page 4 to guide your search and to understand a map's pictorial language.

- Use a magnifying glass to take a deeper dive and get lost in the art and science of cartography.

- Some challenges are listed with an asterisk (*) to indicate duplicate locations on a map. Remember to seek for multiple coordinates!

- Note that all lakes and creeks are spelled as they appear on the map.

- Under the State Parks & Rec. category, State Forests will carry a suffix of S.F., State Recreation Areas have an S.R.A. suffix but State Parks will not carry a suffix.

Check Your Work

Want to see if you've got it right? Are you stumped? Turn to pages 54-64 for puzzle solutions.

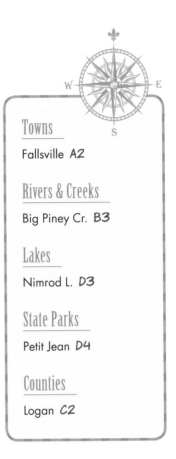

Towns

Fallsville **A2**

Rivers & Creeks

Big Piney Cr. **B3**

Lakes

Nimrod L. **D3**

State Parks

Petit Jean **D4**

Counties

Logan **C2**

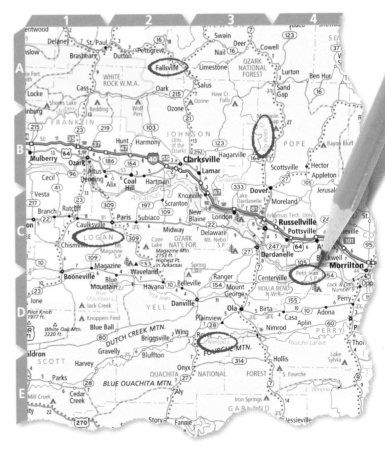

Alabama The Yellowhammer State

In Oak Grove, Alabama, there is a hill at the intersection of Old Hwy 280 and Gravity Road where the gravity is defied. Cars positioned south at the bottom, with the hill in the rearview mirror, parked in neutral, foot off the break, will roll backward and uphill. Yep. It's true and you'll want to drive it more than once.

Know what else you'll want to do after Gravity Hill?

Tour Alabama's beautiful gulf coastline, explore its Appalachian Mountains, its millions of acres of forest lands, its one-of-a-kind meteorite crater and its significant landmarks from the American Civil Rights Movement.

How to *Map It!*™ Use the list below to seek a challenge found on the map. Once found, circle or highlight, then jot down the map coordinates next to the listed challenge to mark it as solved (see sample.) Coordinates can be found using the letter and number grids that frame the map.

Towns

Oak Grove *C6*
Alexander City
America
Barfield
Buhl
Burnt Corn
Calcis
Chestnut
Corona
Fairview
Friendship
Gorgas
Havana
Jenifer
Lawley
Marvel
Mount Olive
Mt. Olive
New London
Paul

Pine Level
Omega
Orion
Salitpa
Six Mile
Snow Hill
Thornton
Unity
Waldo
White Plains

Rivers & Creeks

Big Escambia Cr.
Black Warrior
Cedar Cr.
Coosa
Little R.
Mulberry Cr.
Pea River
Pigeon Cr.
Pintlala Cr.

*Multiple coordinates

Sepulga
Sipsey River
Tombigbee

Lakes

Bankhead L.
Conecuh
Gantt L.
Jordon Lake
L. Mitchell
L. Tuscaloosa
Lake Demopolis
Lake Tholocco
Lay Lake
Logan Martin L.
Martin Lake

Villes

Adamsville
Belleville
Brantleyville
Centerville
Clintonville
Davisville
Deatsville
Elamville
Farmersville
Goldville
Gordonsville
Holtville
Johnstonville
Lineville
Maplesville
Millerville
Newtonville
Plantersville*
Suggsville
Wagarville

Counties

Bibb
Clarke
Coffee
Conecuh
Covington
Dallas
Escambia
Fayette
Greene
Hale
Jefferson
Lowndes
Macon
Marengo
Perry
Pike
St. Clair
Talladega
Tallapoosa

Puzzle solutions, pages 54-64

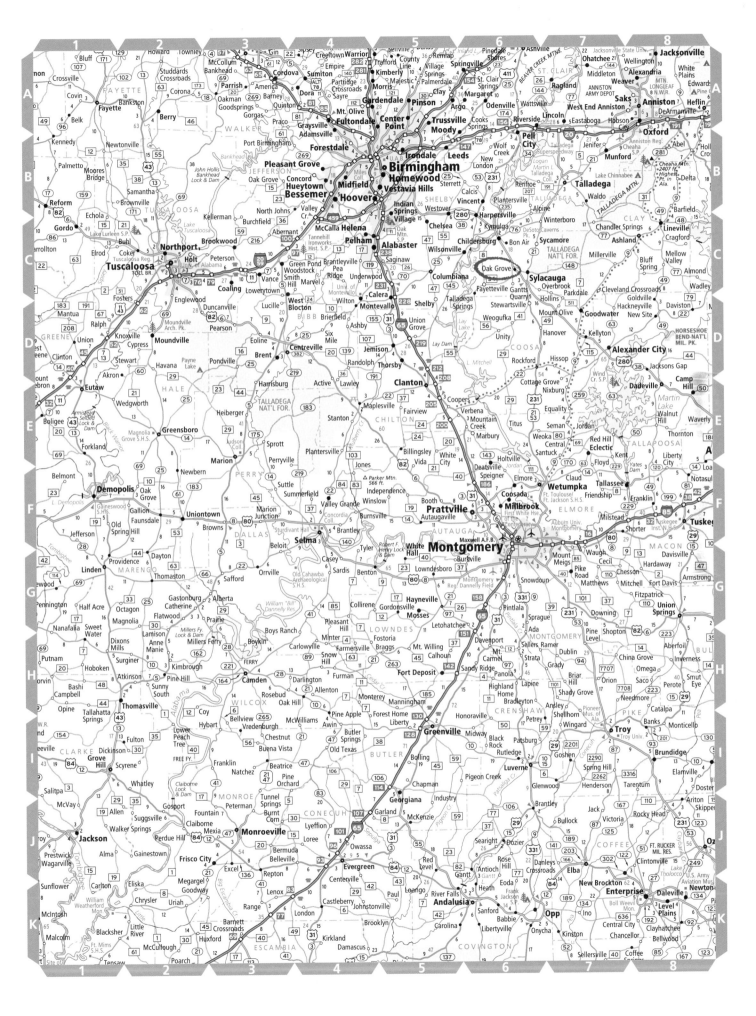

Arizona The Grand Canyon State

Of course the Grand Canyon is a must-see in Arizona, but what about another destination on a grand scale? In the Sonoran Desert, outside Tucson, is the "Boneyard"—a field of 4,000+ old military and NASA aircraft from WWII to the present that you can tour. Turns out desert air is good for people and planes. What else is good in Arizona? Everything!

Enjoy every inch of Arizona from the northern forests filled with pine, fir and spruce trees, to Native American reservations, mountain ranges and ski resorts, to desert areas and resort cities.

How to Map It!™ Use the list below to seek a challenge found on the map. Once found, circle or highlight, then jot down the map coordinates next to the listed challenge to mark it as solved (see sample.) Coordinates can be found using the letter and number grids that frame the map.

Towns

Why K1
Cherry
Comobabi
Dragoon
Fort Apache
Friendly Corners
Geronimo
Indian Pine
Kirkland
La Palma
Picacho
Punkin Center
Rillito
Rock Springs
Strawberry
Theba
Tortilla Flat
Turkey Flat
Valle
Young

Rivers & Creeks

Agua Fria
Aravaipa Cr.
Big Bonito Cr.
Big Chino Wash
Canyon Cr.
Cherry Cr.
Clear Cr.
Cottonwood Wash
Gila*
Hassayampa
Little Colorado*
N. Fk. White
Quilotosa Wash.
Salt
San Carlos
San Pedro
Tonto Cr.
White

*Multiple coordinates

Lakes

Apache L.
Bartlett Res.
Blue Ridge Res.
Chevelon Canyon L.
Horseshoe Res.
L. Pleasant
Mormon L.
San Carlos Res.
Theodore Roosevelt Lake

Counties

Cochise
Maricopa
Navajo
Pima
Yavapai

State Parks & Rec

Boyce Thompson Arboretum
Catalina
Dead Horse Ranch
Fool Hollow Lake Rec. Area
Ft. Verde St. Hist. Pk.
Granite Mtn. Hotshots Memorial
Homolovi
Lost Dutchman
McFarland St. Hist. Pk.
Oracle
Picacho Peak
Red Rock
Roper Lake
Slide Rock
Tonto Natural Bridge

Camp Sites

Blue Ridge
Chevelon Lake
Christopher Cr.
Dairy Springs
Granite Basin
Kaibab Lake
Kinnikinick Lake
Lakeside
Manzanita
Pinegrove
Ponderosa
Rock Crossing
Rose Canyon
Soldier Creek
Spencer Canyon
Tortilla
White Spar
Wolf Cr.

Puzzle solutions, pages 54-64

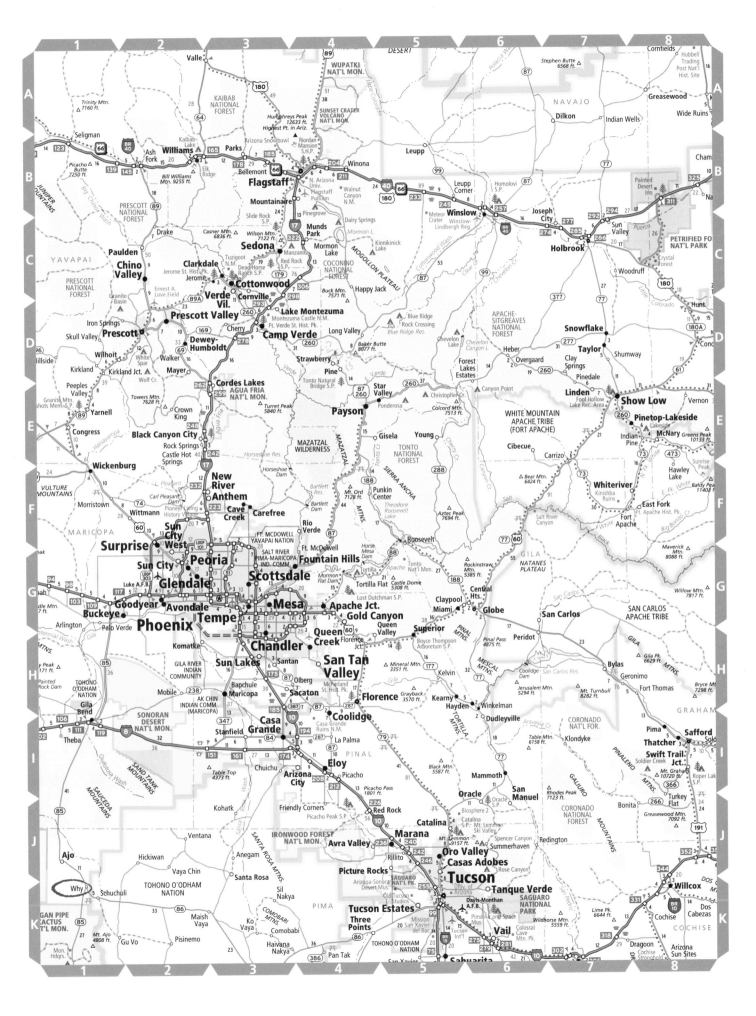

Arkansas The Natural State

Talk about a gem of a state. Did you know if you find a diamond in Arkansas's Crater of Diamonds State Park you can keep it? It's true! So is the fact that Arkansas is filled with charming towns, park and wilderness areas, mountains, caves, rivers and hot springs to explore.

How to *Map It!*™ *Use the list below to seek a challenge found on the map. Once found, circle or highlight, then jot down the map coordinates next to the listed challenge to mark it as solved (see sample.) Coordinates can be found using the letter and number grids that frame the map.*

Towns	Rivers & Creeks	Lakes	State Parks & Rec	Counties
Big Fork *F1*	Arkansas	Blue Mountain L.	Cane Cr.	Ashley
Blackwell	Bayou Bartholomew	Dardanelle L.	Crater of Diamonds	Clark
Cecil	Bayou des Arc	Degray L.	Daisy	Drew
Columbus	Big Piney Cr.	L. Conway	Historic Washington	Franklin
Floral	Cadron	L. Erling	Jenkins Ferry	Garland
Formosa	Cutoff	L. Greeson	Lake Catherine	Grant
Harmony	Fourche LaFave	L. Maumelle	Lake Dardanelle	Hempstead
Hattieville	Little Missouri	L. Ouachita	Lake Ouachita	Hot Springs
Holly Springs	Little Red	L. Winona	Logoly	Jefferson
Ladd	Moro Cr.	Little Red	Lower White River Mus.	Lafayette
Lisbon	Ouachita	Millwood L.	Marks' Mill	Lonoke
Okolona	Petite Jean	Ozark L.	Moro Bay	Miller
Perrytown	Red	Peckerwood L.	Mt. Magazine	Perry
Providence	Saline	White Oak L.	Mt. Nebo	Pike
Saratoga	S. Fk. Little Red		Petite Jean	Pope
St. Vincent	Smackover Cr.		Pinnacle Mtn.	Pulasky
Tulid			Plantation Agri. Mus.	Saline
Tyro			Poison Spr.	Scott
Wright			Toltec Mnds. Archeological	Yell
Yorktown			White Oak Lake	
			Woolly Hollow	

W   E

S

Puzzle solutions, pages 54-64

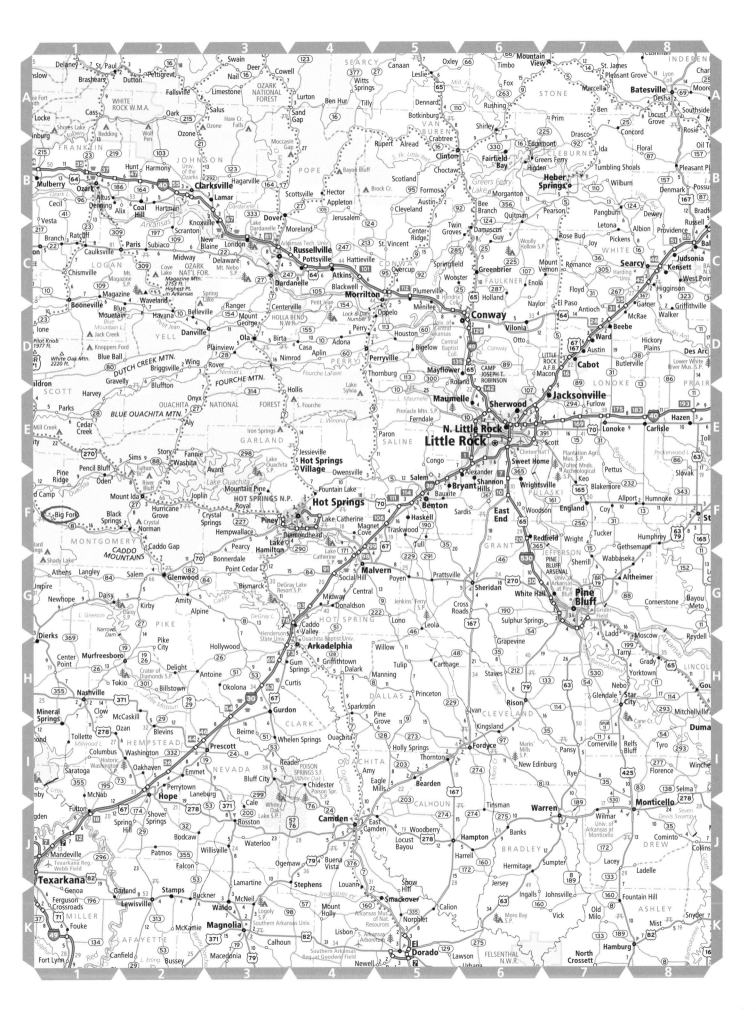

California The Golden State

Do you feel like you're making a difference when you recycle? In Fort Bragg, CA, Mother Nature has made a huge difference recycling at Glass Beach. For decades the pounding, saltwater waves and tidal action of the Pacific Ocean have been crushing and polishing trash once dumped on the beach. The result? A shoreline covered with millions of pieces of smooth sea glass in a rainbow of colors. Recycled, resurfaced and really amazing.

Mother Nature has also blessed California with much more to enjoy—an array of national parks, volcanoes and vineyards and redwood forests, snow skiing, beaches and desert, and museums and big exciting cities—and some of the best tacos anywhere.

How to Map It!™ Use the list below to seek a challenge found on the map. Once found, circle or highlight, then jot down the map coordinates next to the listed challenge to mark it as solved (see sample.) Coordinates can be found using the letter and number grids that frame the map.

Towns	Villes	Lakes	Valleys	Rivers & Creeks
Fort Bragg E1	Boonville	Bear	Browns Valley	Black Butte
Caribou	Bridgeville	Black Butte Lake	Castro Valley	Butte Cr.*
Crows Landing	Collinsville	Bucks L.	Garden Valley	Cache Cr.
Drytown	Dairyville	Camanche Res.	Grass Valley	Calaveras
Eel Rock	Forestville	Clear L.	Hidden Valley	Deer Cr.
Gold Run	Granitevillle	Eagle Lake	Meadow Valley	Dry Cr.
Hopland	Geyserville	L. Berryessa	Mill Valley	Eel*
Knights Landing	Janesville	L. Davis	Penn Valley	Garcia
Navarro	Kelseyville	L. Pillsbury	Pope Valley	Hayfork Cr.
Occidental	Laytonville	L. Sonoma	Potter Valley	Littlejohns Cr.
Rough & Ready	Millville	Lake Almanor	Redwood Valley	Mad
Sheep Ranch	Oakville	Lake Oroville	Strawberry Valley	Pine Cr.
Tomales	Placerville	Modesto Res.	Valley Ford	Rubicon
Viola	Roseville	New Melones L.	Valley Home	Silver Cr.
Waterloo	Smartville	Pardee Res.	Valley Springs	Trinity
Yolo	Taylorsville	Turlock L.		Yuba
Zenia				

*Multiple coordinates

Puzzle solutions, pages 54-64

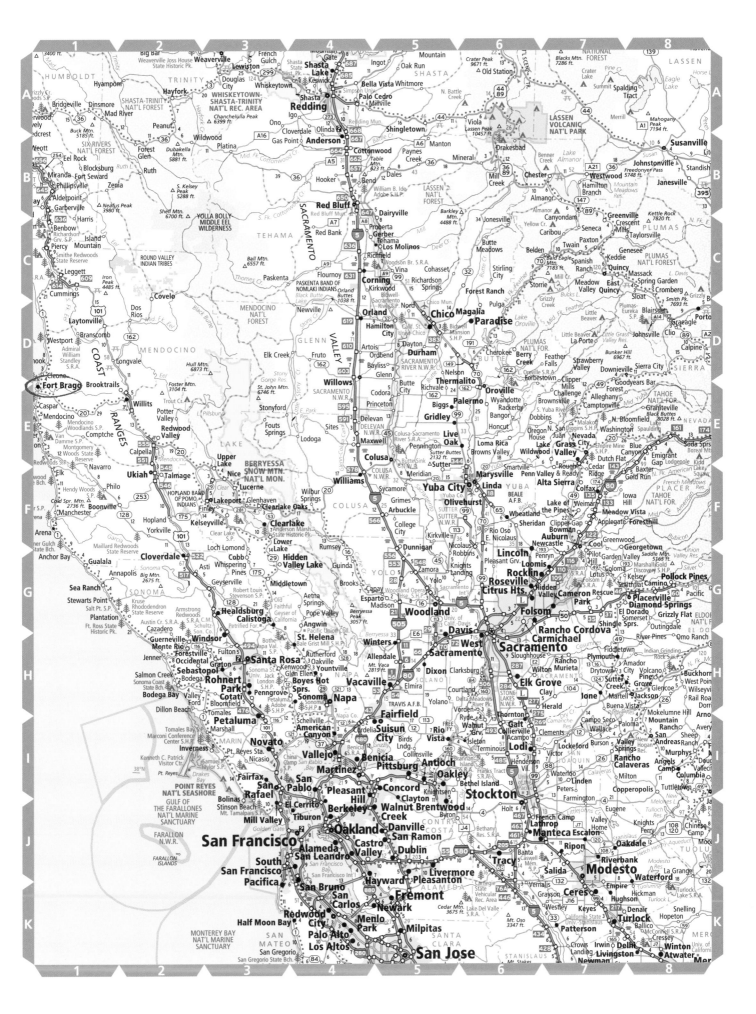

Colorado The Centennial State

You can't help but look up in this mountainous state. But when you're bravely standing on the deck of Royal Gorge Bridge in Cañon City, Colorado, you'll be looking 956 feet down to the valley floor. Once the highest bridge in the world, this wood plank construction stretches 880 feet across the Royal Gorge and cost just $350,000 back in 1929.

Gain even more Colorado perspectives exploring the state's arid desert areas, river canyons, snow covered peaks and ski towns, Ancient Pueblo cliff dwellings and modern, downtown Denver.

How to Map It!™ Use the list below to seek a challenge found on the map. Once found, circle or highlight, then jot down the map coordinates next to the listed challenge to mark it as solved (see sample.) Coordinates can be found using the letter and number grids that frame the map.

Towns

Cañon City **H6**
Beulah
Boone
Campion
Coalmont
Eldora
Gilman
Goldfield
Gould
Heeney
Hygiene
Jefferson
La Garita
Louviers
Milner
Niwot
Ohio
Powderhorn
Red Wing
Tabernash
Tincup
Watkins
Whitepine

Rivers & Creeks

Big Thompson
Blue
Box Elder Cr.
Colorado
Cucharas
Eagle
Fraser
Fryingpan
Grape Cr.
Huerfano
Illinois
Kiowa Cr.
Rio Grande
Saguache Cr.
San Luis Cr.
S. Platte
St. Charles
Tarryall Cr.
Taylor
Tomichi Cr.
Willow

Ski

Beaver Cr.
Buttermilk
Eldora Mtn.
Granby Ranch
Howelsen Hill
Loveland
Monarch Mtn.
Ski Cooper

Counties

Alamosa
Boulder
Chaffee
Clear Creek
Eagle
Gunnison
Huerfano
Mineral
Park
Rio Grande
Saguache
Teller

State Parks & Rec

Barr Lake
Boyd Lake
Chatfield
Eldorado Canyon
Eleven Mile
Golden Gate Canyon
Lake Pueblo
Lathrop
Lory
Mueller
San Luis
Stagecoach
State Forest
Staunton
St. Vrain
Sylvan Lake

N
NW   NE
W   E
SW   SE
S

Puzzle solutions, pages 54-64

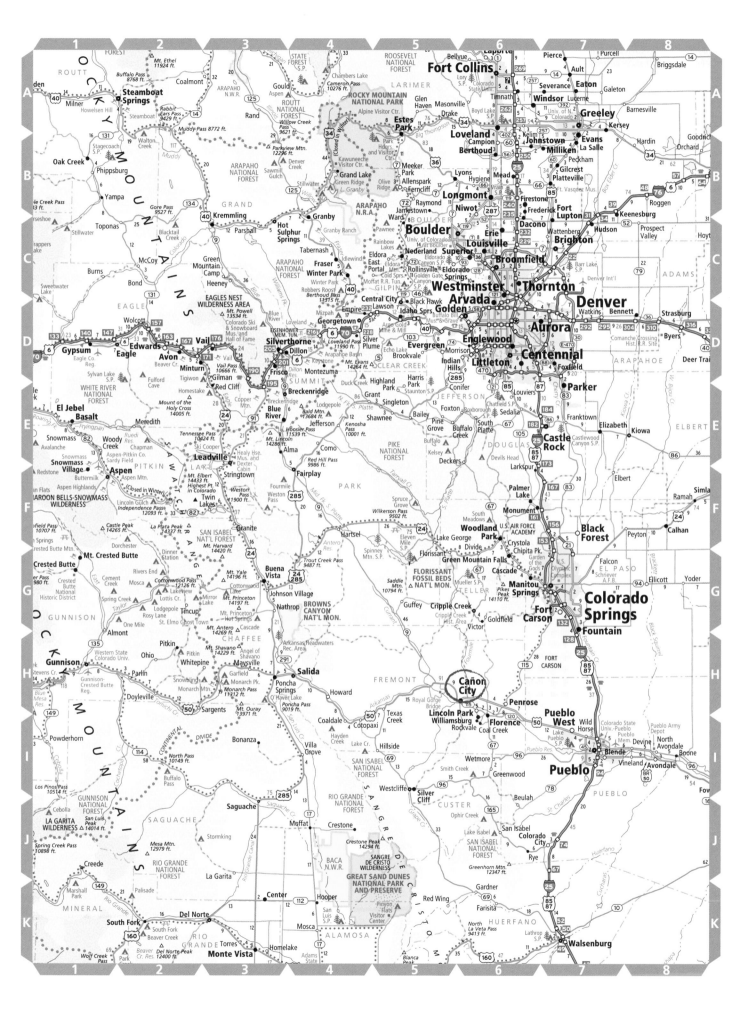

Connecticut The Constitution State

How would you like to taste the first hamburger ever made? Well, a fresher version anyway. Make your way to Louis' Lunch in New Haven, Connecticut and that's what you'll get. How do we know Louis Lassen cooked it first? Because he and the Library of Congress say so. Story goes that sometime around 1900 Louis served a rushed customer some steak trimmings on two pieces of toast—bada bing—the first hamburger. Order up!

After lunch with Louis, make time to make your way around Connecticut's coastal fringes, rural (even volcanic!) parklands and charming New England small towns for which they are so famous.

How to *Map It!*™ Use the list below to seek a challenge found on the map. Once found, circle or highlight, then jot down the map coordinates next to the listed challenge to mark it as solved (see sample.) Coordinates can be found using the letter and number grids that frame the map.

Towns	Rivers & Creeks	Lakes	Villes	State Parks & Rec
New Haven H4	Aspetuck	Amston L.	Amesville	American Legion
Coventry	Bantam	Andover L.	Bakersville	Burr Pond
Easton	Blackberry	Bolton L.	Branchville	Dart Island
Ebbs Corner	Cherry Brook	Broad Brook Res.	Collinsville	Dinosaur
East Granby	Coginchaug	Easton Res.	Hotchkissville	Kettletown
Firetown	Connecticut	Hancock Brook L.	Hazardville	Gay City
Good Hill	Farm	L. Gaillard	Leesville	Housatonic Meadows
Hartland	Farmington	L. Waramaug	Mixville	Indian Well
Long Hill	Hammonasset	Nepaug Res.	Northville	Meshomasic
Marlborough	Housantonic*	Old Marsh Pond	Plantsville	Penwood
Oxford	Mad*	Pickerel L.	Quarryville	Putnam Mem.
Redding	Mill	Pocotopaug L.	Somersville	Scantic River
South Kent	Mattabesset	L. Quassapaug	Unionville	Selden Neck
Southport	Pequonnock	Scoville Res.	Whigville	Silver Sands
West Avon	Saugatuck	Silver L.		Sherwood Island
West Goshen	Stony	Trap Falls Res.		Wharton Brook
Woodtick	Willimantic	Twin Lakes		
		Wangumbaug L.		

*Multiple coordinates

N
NW   NE
W   E
SW   SE
S

Puzzle solutions, pages 54-64

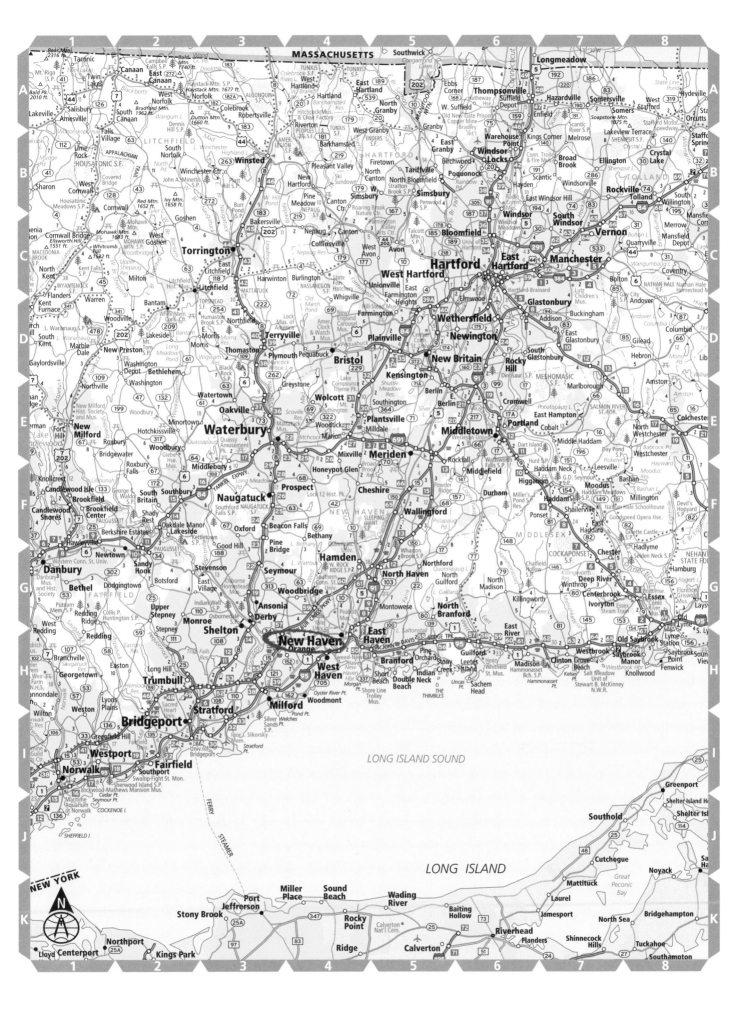

Florida The Sunshine State

Mermaids are a myth. Or are they? In Florida's Weeki Wachee Springs State Park, you'll find North America's deepest, naturally formed spring, where peacocks, manatees, turtles and gators roam and where real-live mermaids have been swimming and dancing below its surface since 1947. Come look for yourself!

And there's plenty more to see from the white sand, gulf-side beaches to the Atlantic shores, to eclectic Miami and quirky Key West, Florida is filled with sunny discoveries.

How to *Map It!™* Use the list below to seek a challenge found on the map. Once found, circle or highlight, then jot down the map coordinates next to the listed challenge to mark it as solved (see sample.) Coordinates can be found using the letter and number grids that frame the map.

Towns

Bayport *G2*
Bellwood
Christmas
Crescent Beach
De Soto City
Emporia
Fellowship
Fort Drum
Frostproof
Keysville
Lake Como
Lisbon
Narcoossee
Orange Mills
Oxford
Ozona
Painters Hill
Summer Haven
Waldo
Weeki Wachee
Yankeetown

*Multiple coordinates

Rivers & Creeks

Hillsborough
Kissimmee
Manatee
Olustee Cr.
Peace
Santa Fe

Lakes

Alligator L.
Blue Cypress Lake
Lake June in Winter
Crooked L.
Kingsley Lake
L. Disston
L. Harris
L. Hart
L. Poinsett
L. Rosalie
L. Sampson
L. Stafford
L. Tarpon

L. Yale
Lake Hellen Blazes
Lake Istokpoga
Lake Marian
Lake Marion
Lake Rousseau
Lake Winder
Levy Lake
Orange L.
Puzzle Lake
Santa Fe L.
Tsala Apopka Lake

State Parks & Rec

Blue Spr.
Bulow Creek
Caladesi Island
Cedar Key Mus.
Chrystal River Arch
Colt Creek
Ft. Cooper
Dade Bfld. Hist

De Leon Sprs.
Fanning Springs
Faver-Dykes
Folk Culture Ctr.
Guana River
Highlands Hammock
Lake Griffin
Lake Louisa
Lake Manatee
Lake Wales Ridge
Peacock Springs
Rainbow Springs
Ravine Gdns
Tomoka
Weeki Wachee Springs
Wekiwa Sprs.
Withlacoochee S.F.*

Counties

Alachua
Citrus
Clay
Columbia
Duval
Gilchrist
Hillsborough
Lake
Manatee
Marion
Orange
Osceola
Pasco
Pinellas
Seminol
St. Johns
Sumter
Suwannee
Union

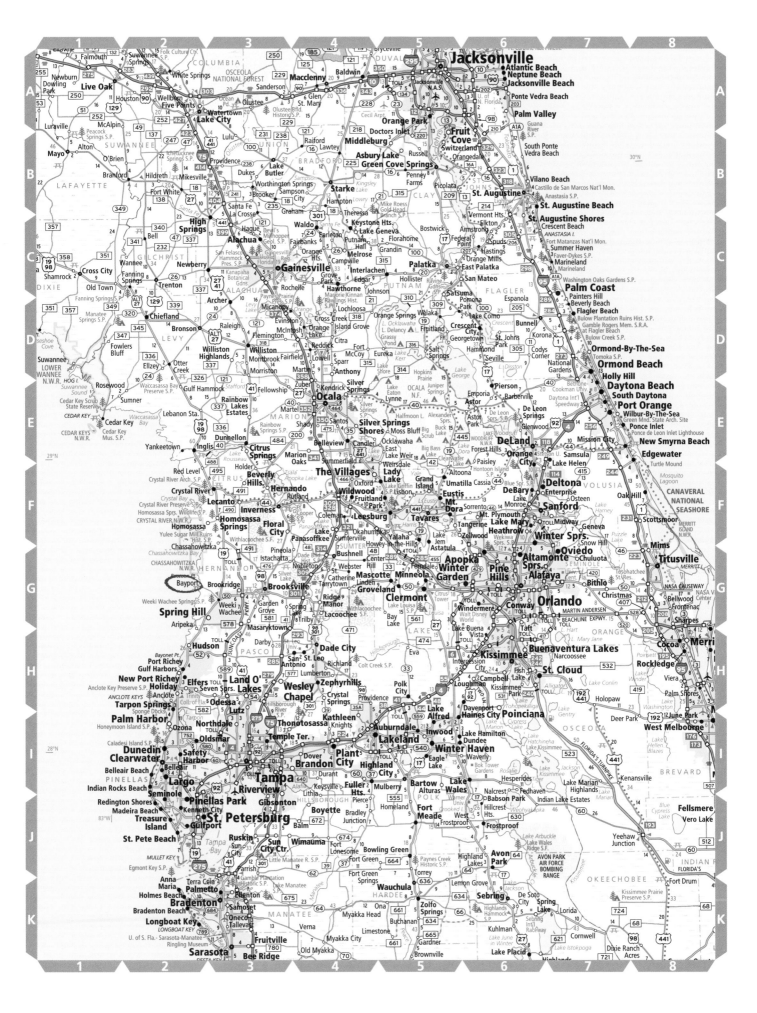

Georgia The Peach State

In Georgia, tunnel vision is wide and green—when you're driving through the mile and a half long, 400+ live-oak-lined Tunnel of Trees that is. Speckled with light and dripping with Spanish moss, this magical Savannah drive takes you down the longest live oak-covered road in the world.

Where else can Georgia take you? From the Atlantic coastal islands, to mossy, low-country swamps, through antebellum towns to mountain vistas, this southern state offers a bit of everything.

How to Map It!™ Use the list below to seek a challenge found on the map. Once found, circle or highlight, then jot down the map coordinates next to the listed challenge to mark it as solved (see sample.) Coordinates can be found using the letter and number grids that frame the map.

Towns	Rivers & Creeks	Villes	State Parks & Rec	Counties
Adrian *G7*	Abrams	Abbeville	Bobby Brown S.R.A.	Bacon
Austell	Big Satilla	Adgateville	F.D.R.	Barrow
Boneville	Broad	Boneville	General Coffee	Ben Hill
Brookfield	Flint	Byromville	Georgia Vet. Mem.	Bibb
Brooklyn	Gum Swamp	Charlotteville	Hamburg	Carroll
Dooling	Kinchafoonee Cr.	Danville	High Falls	Clay
Fortsonia	Little Ohoopee	Draneville	Indian Sprs.	Clayton
Good Hope	Muckalee Cr.	Ellaville	Kolomoki Mnds.	Cobb
Lilly	Ocmulgee	Hollonville	Little Ocmulgee	De Kalb
Lizella	Pataula Cr.	Irwinville	Mistletoe	Dooly
Pine Grove	Satilla	Luthersville	Panola Mtn.	Lamar
Potterville	South	Meansville	Red Top Mtn.	Lincoln
Round Oak	Spring	Ruckersville	Richard B. Russell	Meriwether
Salem	Upatoi	Smithville	Sweetwater Cr.	Oconee
Sand Hill	Yellow	Snipesville	Watson Mill Br.	Peach
Stewart		Starrsville	Will-A-Way S.R.A.	Pike
The Rock		Watkinsville		Rockdale
Upton				Tift
Youth				Treutlen
Vanna				

W   E

S

Puzzle solutions, pages 54-64

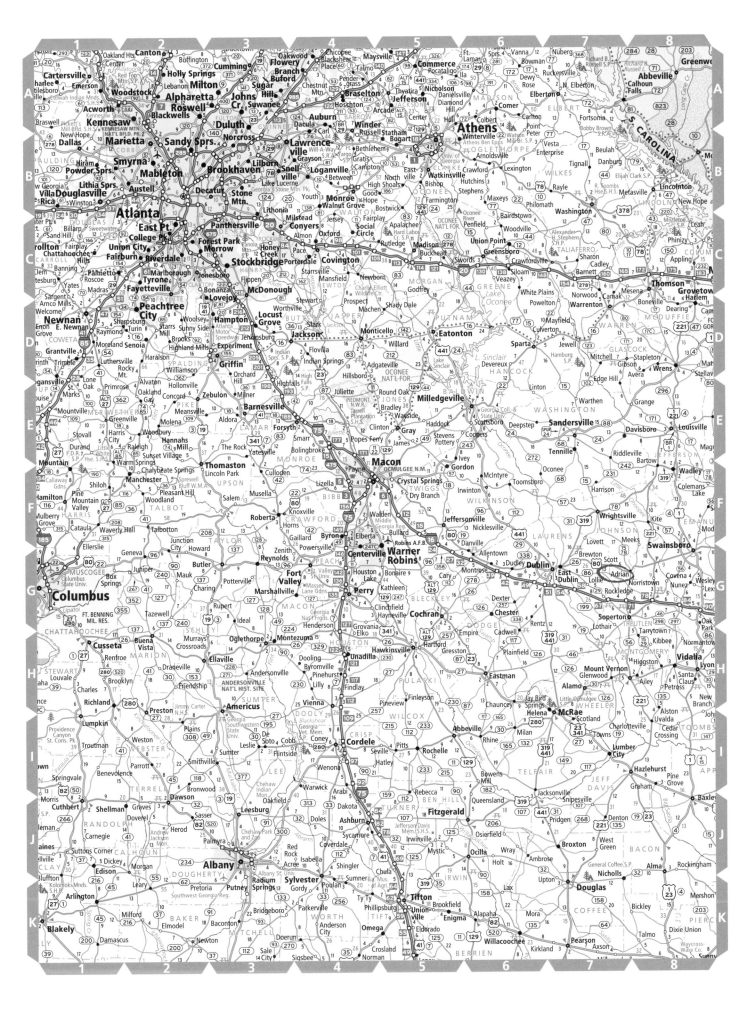

Idaho The Gem State

Are you in Idaho or on the moon? When you're hiking Craters of the Moon National Monument & Preserve along the Great Rift of Idaho, it's hard to tell. A foreign, moon-like landscape, Craters evolved over volcanic eruptions started 15,000 years ago. Apollo astronauts explored its vast sea of black lava flows, tubes, caves and cones, in preparation for their trips into space and you can, too.

After the moon, there are plenty more giant steps to take in Idaho from mountainous landscapes and Sun Valley skiing to its many protected wilderness areas like Yellowstone National Park, to city life in Boise and Coeur d'Alene.

How to *Map It!*™ *Use the list below to seek a challenge found on the map. Once found, circle or highlight, then jot down the map coordinates next to the listed challenge to mark it as solved (see sample.) Coordinates can be found using the letter and number grids that frame the map.*

Towns	Rivers & Creeks	Lakes	State Parks & Rec	Counties
Bliss J4	Battle Cr.	Arrowrock Res.	Bruneau Dunes	Adams
Boise	Big Lost*	Blackfoot Res.	Craters of the Moon Nat'l Mon. and Preserve	Bingham
Bone	Birch Cr.	Cedar Creek Res.		Boise
Butte City	Castle Cr.	Deadwood Res.	Dworshak	Clearwater
Cobalt	Goose Cr.	Hells Canyon Res.	Eagle Island	Custer
Crouch	Jarbridge	Lake Cascade	Earl M. Hardy Box Canyon Sprs. Pres.	Elmore
Eden	Kelly	Mud L.		Gem
Golden	Lawyer	Paddock Valley Res.	Heyburn	Gooding
St. Joe	Little Lost	Payette L.	Lake Cascade	Idaho
King Hill	Loon	Ririe Res.	Lake Walcott	Jefferson
Lucile	Meadow Cr.		Land of Yankee Fork	Lemhi
Magic City	Medicine Lodge		Lucky Peak	Lewis
Mud Lake	Owyhee	**Ski**	Malad Gorge	Power
Princeton	Panther Cr.		Mary Minerva McCroskey	Shoshone
Swanlake	Reynolds	Brundage Mtm.	Ponderosa	Valley
Thornton	Selway	Little Ski Hill	Three Island Crossing	
Waha	Snake*	Pomerelle Mtn.	Winchester Lake	
		Soldier Mountain		
		Sun Valley		

Multiple coordinates

Puzzle solutions, pages 54-64

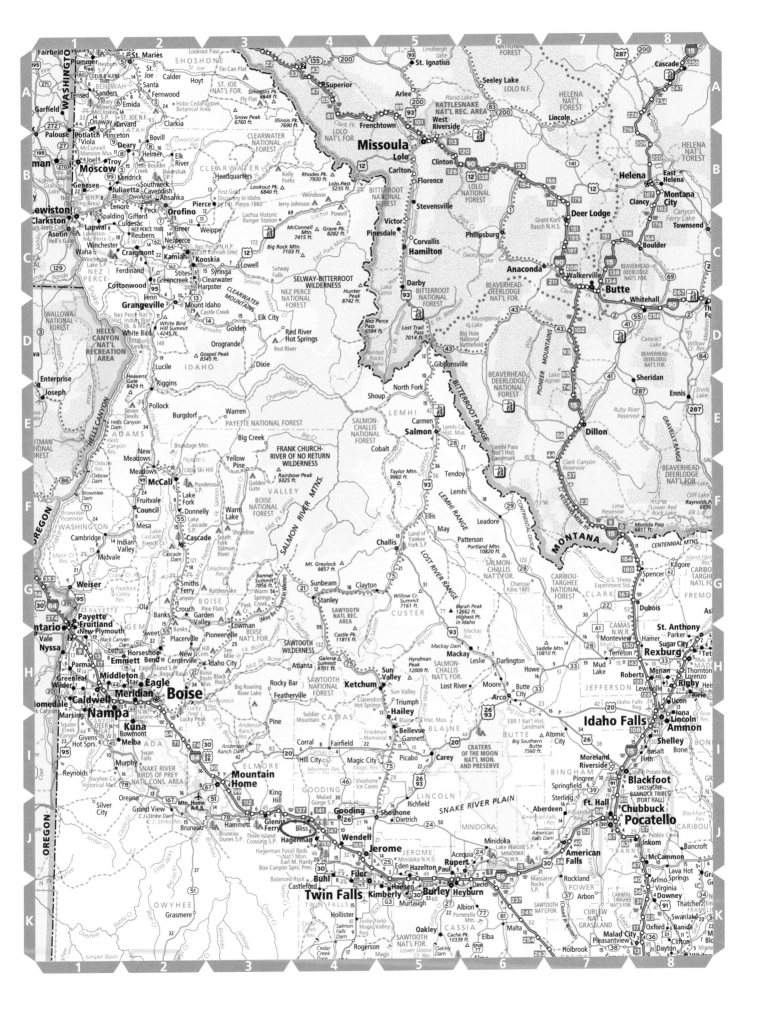

Illinois *The Prairie State*

You've seen one squirrel; you've seen 'em all, right? Not in Olney, Illinois. Olney is home to rare albino squirrels. Their white squirrel likenesses can be seen on Olney police cars and parks and crossing signs. By law, they have the right of way on public streets. Olney City Park, in early morning, is said to be best for squirrel sightings. If you miss them, the bakery can serve you a white squirrel cookie.

There are plenty of other Illinois-only wonders. From Chicago to Lincoln's Library in Springfield to great towns along the Mississippi River, Illinois is filled with one-of-a-kind adventures.

How to Map It!™ *Use the list below to seek a challenge found on the map. Once found, circle or highlight, then jot down the map coordinates next to the listed challenge to mark it as solved (see sample.) Coordinates can be found using the letter and number grids that frame the map.*

Towns

Olney J8
Berry*
Bible Grove
Bone Gap
Boulder
Bourbon
Cameron
Cuba
Fancy Prairie
Funks Grove
Green Valley
Havana
Kansas
Little America
Loogootee
New Delhi
Panama
Pocahontas
Salisbury
Speer
Trivoli

Multiple coordinates

Rivers & Creeks

Big Muddy
Bonpas Cr.
Kaskaskia*
Little Wabash
Mackinaw
Macoupin Cr.
Mid. Fk. Vermilion
N. Fk. Embarras
Otter Cr.
Salt Cr.
Sangamon
Shoal Cr.
Vermilion

Points of Interest

Lincoln Home N.H.S.
Lincoln Log Cabin
    S.H.S.
Railway Mus.
Rockwell Mound
Rte. 66 Mus.

Lakes

Coffeen L.
East Fork L.
Evergreen L.
Highland Silver L.
Lake Bloomington
L. Charleston
L. Chautauqua
L. Clinton
L. Glenn Shoals
L. Jacksonville
L. Lou Yaeger
L. Mattoon
L. Sara
Lake Shelbyville
L. Springfield
Mound L.
Newton L.
Otter L.
Spoon L.
Spring L.
Stewart L.

State Parks & Rec

Beaver Dam
Clinton Lake S.R.A.
Eldon Hazlet S.R.A.
Fox Ridge
Jubilee Coll.
Moraine View S.R.A.
Ramsey Lake S.R.A.
Rock Island State Tr.
Sand Ridge S.F.
Sangchris Lake
South Shore
Stephen A. Forbes
    S.R.A.
Walnut Pt.
Wildlife Prairie
Wolf Creek

Counties

Christian
Clay
Coles
Douglas
Edwards
Fulton
Greene
Jersey
Logan
Macoupin
McLean
Peoria
Richland
Sangamon
St. Clair
Tazewell
Wayne
Woodford

W · E · S

Puzzle solutions, pages 54-64

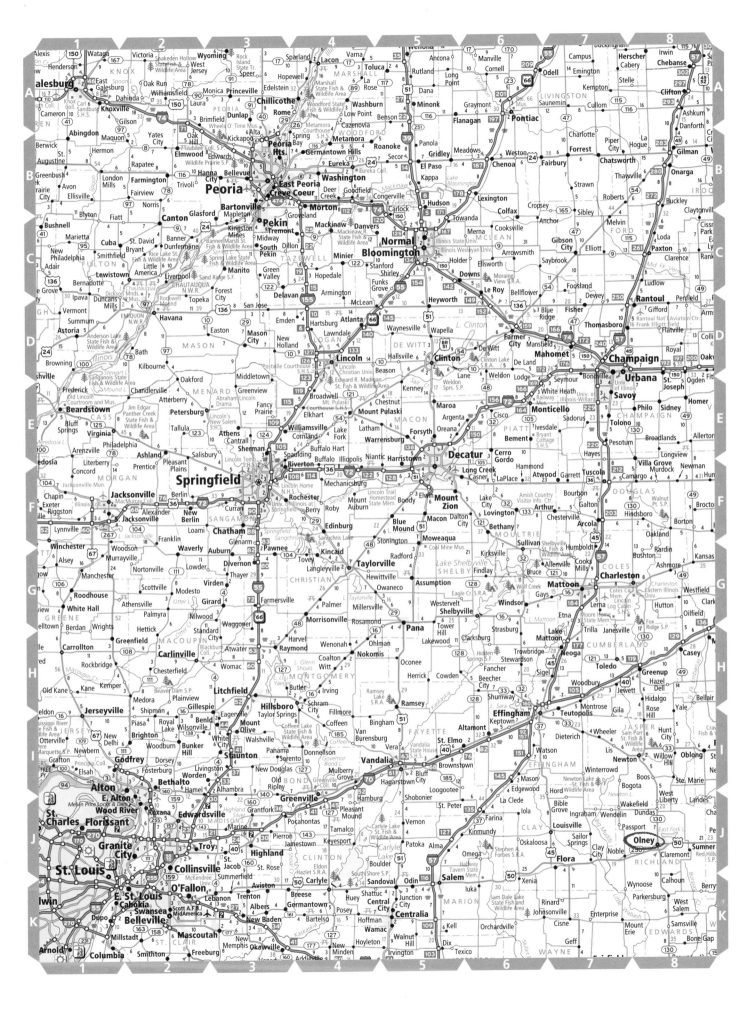

Indiana The Hoosier State

If you thought South Bend, Indiana was all about college football, think again. Right smack in the middle of downtown flows a man-made waterway where Olympic whitewater kayakers train. Constructed in the 1840s to power a sawmill, today the East Race Waterway is about a 2,000–foot ride that any adventurer with a canoe or kayak can take. What other thrills await?

From giant sand dunes and miles of Lake Michigan shoreline, to the roar of the race cars, to hiking Indiana's grand canyon, there's plenty to keep you happy in the Hoosier State.

How to Map It!™ *Use the list below to seek a challenge found on the map. Once found, circle or highlight, then jot down the map coordinates next to the listed challenge to mark it as solved (see sample.) Coordinates can be found using the letter and number grids that frame the map.*

Towns

Bakers Corner **D5**
Alert
Cataract
Cincinnati
Eden
Flat Rock
Gnaw Bone
Hall
Leisure
London
Midland
Nineveh
Omega
Pine Village
Raccoon
Rob Roy
Samaria
Wawpecong
Young America

*Multiple coordinates

Rivers & Creeks

Beanblossom Cr.
Big Cr.
Big Blue
Big Raccoon Cr.
Big Walnut Cr.
Driftwood
Eel
Fall Cr.
First
Flatrock
Mill Creek
Salt Cr.
Sand Cr.
Sugar Cr.
Wabash
White*
Wildcat Cr.

Villes

Butlerville
Coatesville
Curtisville
Daleville
Elizaville
Gwynneville
Huntsville
Kirksville
Knightsville
Leesville
Noblesville
Petersville
Queensville
Russellville
Russiaville
Scircleville
Smithville
Spearsville
Taylorsville

State Parks & Rec

Brown County
Fairfax S.R.A.
Frances Slocum
  S.R.A.
Ft. Harrison
Greene-Sullivan S.F.
Lieber S.R.A.
McCormick's Creek
Miami S.R.A.
Morgan Monroe S.F.
Mounds
Paynetown S.R.A.
Raccoon S.R.A.

Counties

Benton
Boone
Clay
Decatur
Fountain
Grant
Greene
Hamilton
Henry
Jennings
Lawrence
Marion
Miami
Owen
Parke
Putnam
Shelby
Tippecanoe

Puzzle solutions, pages 54-64

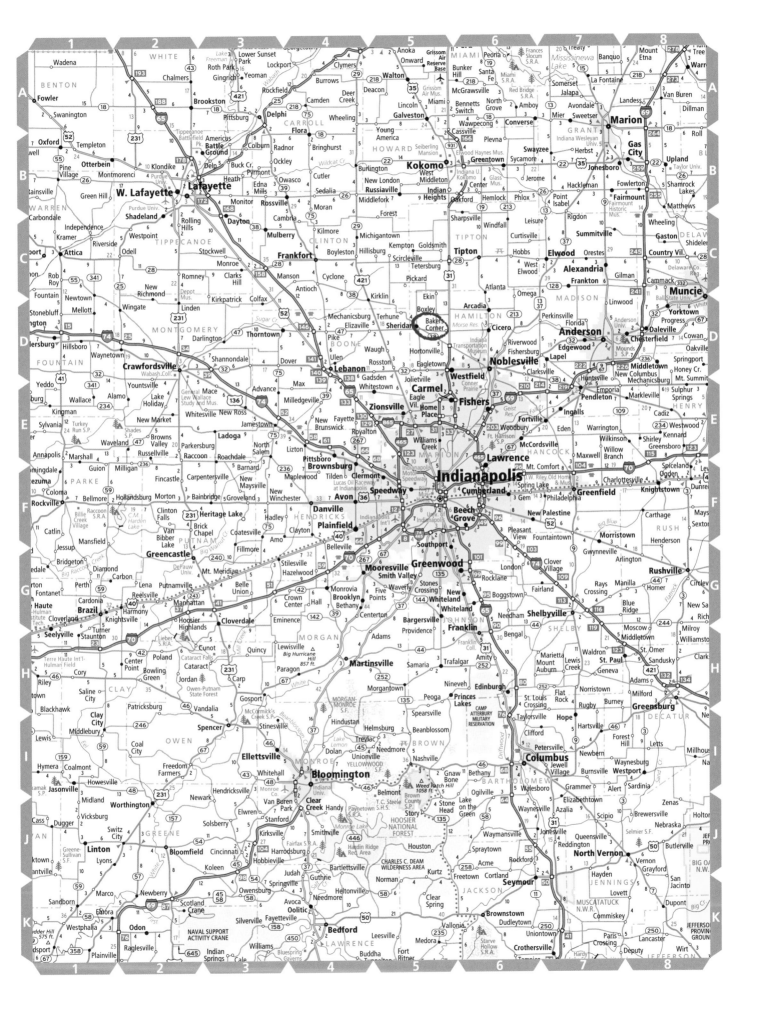

Iowa The Hawkeye State

Are you an art lover? In Iowa art is big, literally. Mt. Vernon is home to the American Gothic Barn—a great, big-as-the-side-of-a-barn, rendering of Iowa native artist Grant Wood's famous farm couple and their pitchfork. You can't miss it. Just like you can't miss the spray-painted recreation of the Sistine Chapel on the ceiling and walls of Galleria de Paco in Waterloo. What other beauty is there to behold?

Iowa is bordered by the mighty Mississippi and Missouri rivers. In between, among the wetlands, rolling plains and cornfields, you'll find prehistoric burial mounds, Madison County's covered bridges, the Field of Dreams— and that's just the tip of the corn stalk.

How to Map It!™ Use the list below to seek a challenge found on the map. Once found, circle or highlight, then jot down the map coordinates next to the listed challenge to mark it as solved (see sample.) Coordinates can be found using the letter and number grids that frame the map.

Towns	Rivers & Creeks	Lakes	State Parks & Rec	Counties
Waterloo *C7*	Beaver	Bays Branch L.	Beeds Lake	Appanoose
Alpha	Black Hawk Cr.	Big Wall Lake	Big Creek	Bremer
Batavia	Boone	East Twin Lake	Bushy Creek St. Rec Area	Butler
Cambria	Buck	Elm Lake	Elk Rock	Decatur
Churchville	Cedar*	Lake Cornelia	George Wyth Mem	Fayette
Dana	Des Moines*	Lake Red Rock	Holst S.F.	Floyd
Evans	E. Fk. Des Moines*	Little Wall L.	Honey Creek	Hardin
Fern	Fox	Morse L.	Lake Ahquabi	Humboldt
Holbrook	Iowa*	Rathbun Lake	Lake Keomah	Iowa
Homer	Middle	Rock Creek L.	Lake Wapello	Jasper
Irving	N. English	Saylorville L.	Ledges	Keokuk
New Virginia	N. Skunk	West Twin Lake	Nine Eagles	Lucas
Ollie	Raccoon		Pine Lake	Madison
Plano	S. Skunk*		Red Haw	Mahaska
Thor	Shell Rock		Rock Creek	Polk
Van Cleve	Wapsipinicon		Shimek S.F.	Story
Westgate	White Breast Cr.		Stephens S.F.	Van Buren
What Cheer	Wolf Cr.		Union Grove	Wapello
Zaneta				Warren

*Multiple coordinates

Puzzle solutions, pages 54-64

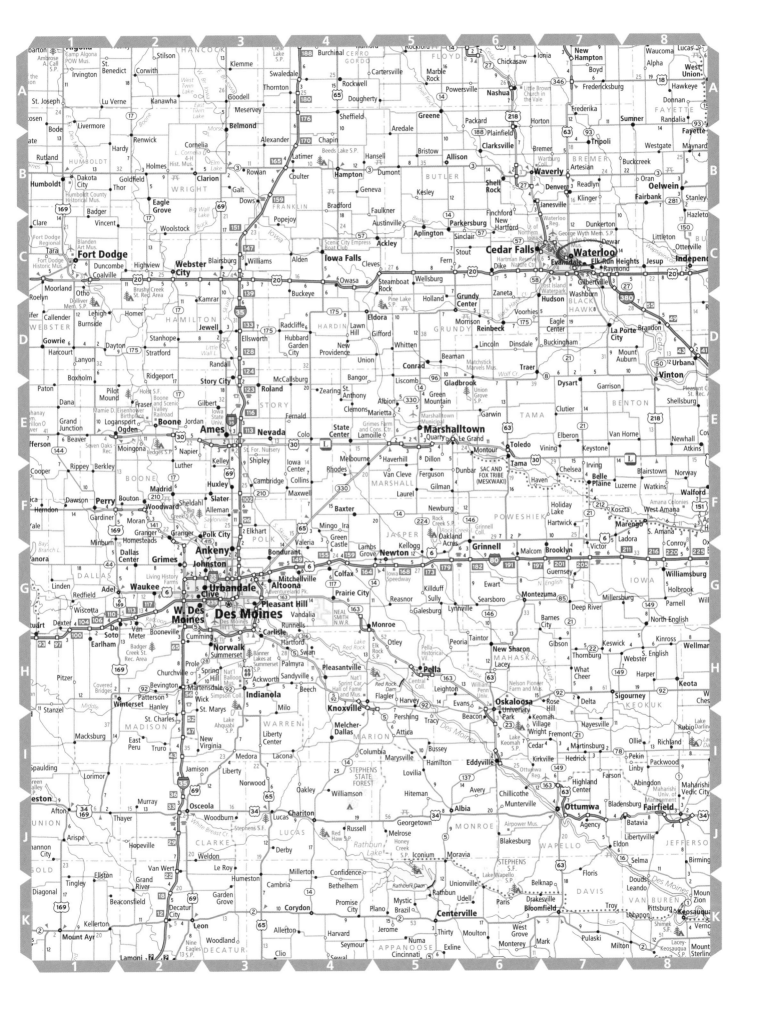

Kansas The Sunflower State

"Hello, hello"...ever yell down a well and wonder if anyone hears you? In Kansas you can climb 136 stairs and 109 feet down into Greensburg's "The Big Well." Dug by hand by local farmers and cowboy types in 1887, this 32-foot wide giant well that was once a water source was almost destroyed by a tornado, and is now a museum where you can go to the bottom and yell "hello" back to the top.

There's no place like Kansas...it is true American heartland with its vast Great Plains, buffalo herds, rolling fields of wheat, sunflowers and a pioneer spirit that draws you in.

How to Map It!™ *Use the list below to seek a challenge found on the map. Once found, circle or highlight, then jot down the map coordinates next to the listed challenge to mark it as solved (see sample.) Coordinates can be found using the letter and number grids that frame the map.*

Towns

Bazaar *G7*
Corbin
Denmark
Dover
Falun
Furley
Groveland
Hedville
Idana
Lake City
Lamont
Lillis
Lovewell
Navarre
Norwich
Oak Valley
Olpe
Oxford
Sawyer
Talmo
Upland
Waldo
Zenith

Lakes

Cheney Res.
Council Grove Lake
El Dorado Lake
Elk City Lake
Fall River Lake
Kanopolis Lake
Lovewell Res.
Marion Res.
Milford Lake
Toronto Lake
Tuttle Creek Res.*

*Multiple coordinates

Waconda Lake
Wilson Lake

Rivers & Creeks

Big Blue
Bluff Creek
Chapman Cr.
Chikaskia
Fall
Grouse Cr.
Little Arkansas
Lyon
Mill Cr.
Neosho
Saline
Salt Creek
Sand Cr.
Smokey Hill
Soldier Cr.

State Parks & Rec

Cheney
Cross Timbers
El Dorado
Fall River
Glen Elder
Kanopolis
Milford
Sand Hills
Tuttle Creek
Wilson

Points of Interest

Garden of Eden
Geographic Center of the Conterminous U.S.
The World's Largest Ball of Sisal Twine

Counties

Barber
Barton
Elk
Ellsworth
Geary
Harper
Harvey
Jewell
Lyon
Marshall
Mitchell
Nemaha
Reno
Republic
Russell
Saline
Sedgwick

W   E

S

Puzzle solutions, pages 54-64

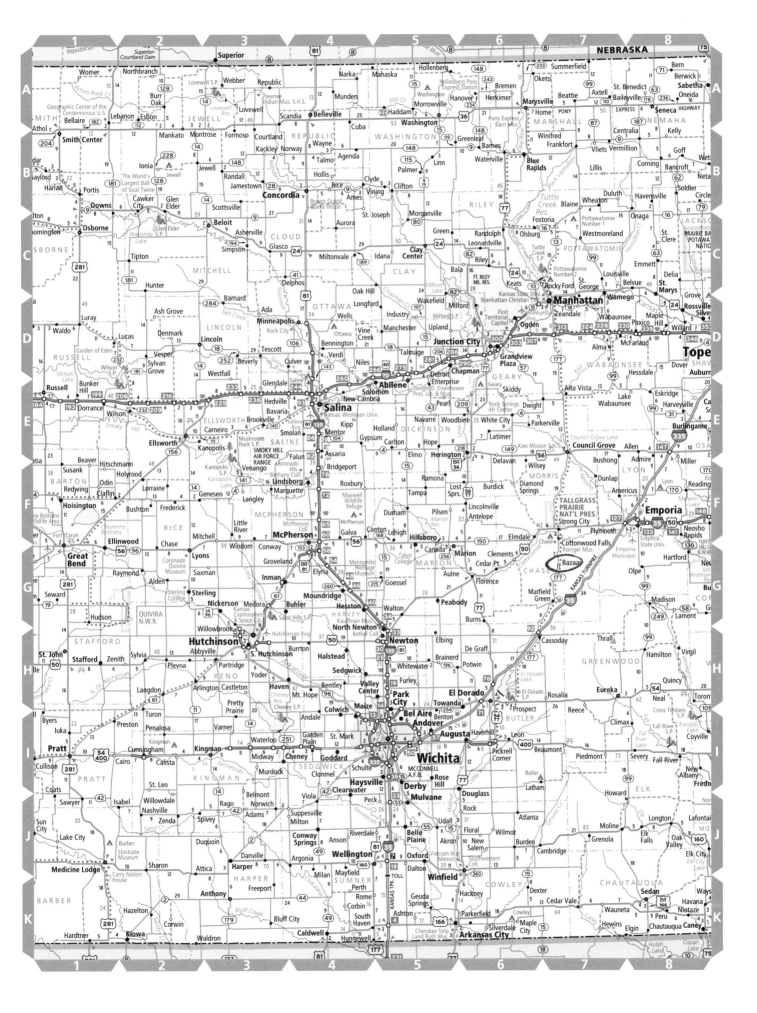

Kentucky The Bluegrass State

Somewhere over the moonbow you'll find Kentucky. Yes, "moonbow"—a lunar rainbow. And Cumberland Falls State Resort Park is one of the few places in the world that has them. Known as "The Niagara of the South" it is where, on a clear night with a full moon above the falls, you can see a rare and magical moonbow. To the naked eye it appears white, but through a camera lens the moonbow's color spectrum is revealed. Unforgettable.

And that's not all y'all. There's the breathtaking Red River Gorge canyon system, Louisville riverboat rides, Kentucky's fifth season of the year "Derby Season", Mammoth Cave, bluegrass music and large glasses of sweet tea, too.

How to *Map It!*™ *Use the list below to seek a challenge found on the map. Once found, circle or highlight, then jot down the map coordinates next to the listed challenge to mark it as solved (see sample.) Coordinates can be found using the letter and number grids that frame the map.*

Towns

Berlin **B5**
Bethany
Black Gnat
Black Snake
Dog Walk
Ella
Gum Sulphur
Holy Cross
Judy
Korea
Lily
Marrowbone
Nevada
Oxford
Rosslyn
Science Hill
Shoulderblade
St. Catharine
Tilton
Vincent

Rivers & Creeks

Beaver*
Big Pitman
Cedar Cr.
Collins Fk.
Drennon
Eagle Cr.
Fleming
Fork Lick
Goose
Green
Houston Cr.
Kentucky*
Kinniconick
Laurel
Little Kentucky
Muddy
Red Bird
Red Lick
Stinking
Stoner Cr.

*Multiple coordinates

Villes

Annville
Booneville
Burkesville
Deatsville
Connersville
Coopersville
Elizaville
Finchville
Gardnersville
Gradyville
Hyattsville
Jacksonville
Kirksville
Minorsville
Mortonsville
Oddville
Owingsville
Pleasureville
Plumville
Preachersville

Royville
Shopville
Southville
Touristville
Worthville

Lakes

Beaver L.
Bullock Pen L.
Cave Run Lake
Green River Lake
Herrington L.
Lake Cumberland
Lake Linville
Laurel River Lake
Taylorsville L.
Williamstown Lake
Wood Creek L.

State Parks & Rec

Big Bone Lick
Blue Licks Battlefield S.R.P.
Buckhorn Lake State Resort Park
Cumberland Falls St. Resort Pk.
General Burnside Island
Kentucky Ridge
Kincaid Lake
Ky. Horse Pk.
Levi Jackson Wilderness Road
My Old Kentucky Home
Natural Bridge State Resort Park
Old Ft. Harrod
Taylorsville Lake

N
NW   *NE*
W   *E*
SW   *SE*
S

Puzzle solutions, pages 54-64

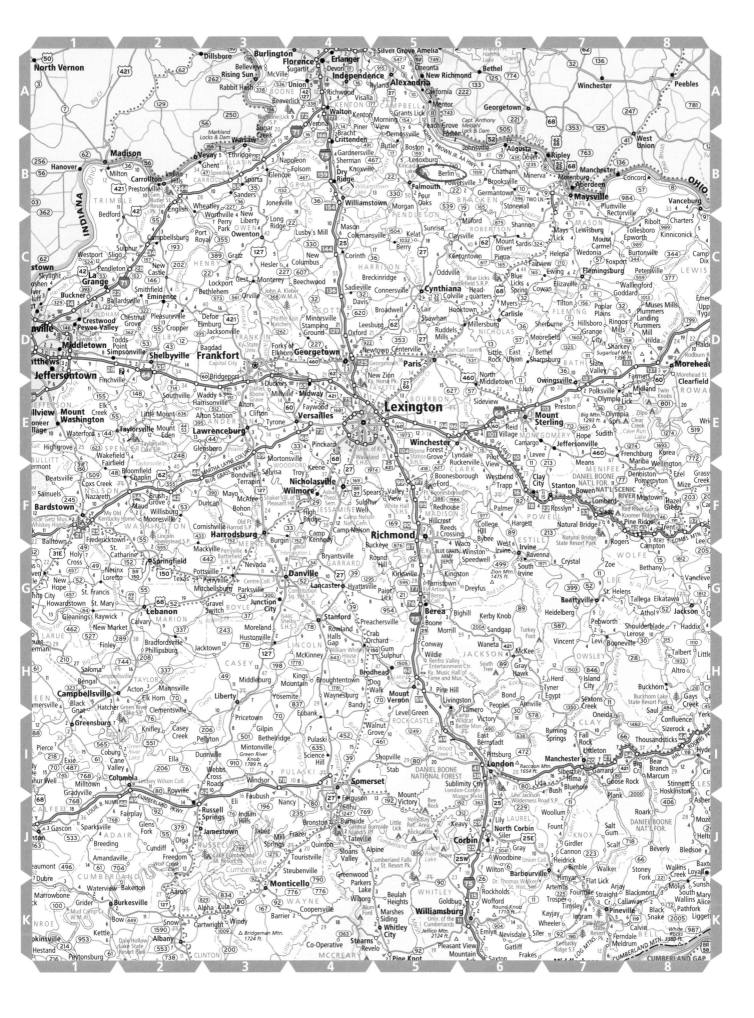

Louisiana The Pelican State

Way down in Louisiana's Atchafalaya [uh chaf uh lie uh] Basin, America's largest wetland swamp, in the town of Pierre Part, is the Cypress Swamp Driftwood Family Museum where "Driftwood Man" uses screws, moss, and googly eyes to give pieces of driftwood a second life as giant creatures, dinos, Big Foots, even a Statue of Liberty. It's totally worth the trip and the artist is glad to show you around.

Like the driftwood, Louisiana is a place where many cultures and traditions create something unique. Swamps, gators, the Mississippi River, history, a music and food paradise, and some of the best folks anywhere make a trip to this state a celebration.

How to Map It!™ *Use the list below to seek a challenge found on the map. Once found, circle or highlight, then jot down the map coordinates next to the listed challenge to mark as solved (see sample.) Coordinates can be found using the letter and number grids that frame the map.*

Towns	Lakes	Rivers & Creeks	Villes	Parishes
Pierre Part *I6*	Black L.	Atchafalaya	Abbeville	Acadia
Aimwell	Bundick Lake	Bayou Anacoco	Bienville	Allen
Bayou Blue	Catahoula L.	Bayou D'Arbonne	Coteau Arnaudville	Bienville
Catahoula	Clear L.	Bayou Macon	Crowville	Concordia
Creole	Cocodrie L.	Bayou Pierre	Deville	De Soto
Dixie Inn	Cotile L.	Bayou San Patricio	Fishville	E. Baton Rouge
Fort Necessity	Grand L.	Black	Haynesville	Evangeline
French Settlement	Kepler Cr. L.	Black L. Bayou	Longville	Grant
Goodwill	L. Bistineau	Boeuf	Marthaville	Iberia
Ivan	L. Boudreaux	Dugdemona	Napoleonville	La Salle
Log Cabin	L. Claiborne	Ouachita	Pineville	Madison
Monticello	L. Iatt	Red	Spearsville	Morehouse
Newlight	L. Misere	Saline Bayou	Springville	Pointe Coupee
Pecan Island	L. Penchant	Tensas	Summerville	Sabine
Pelican	L. St. Joseph	Whisky Chitto Cr.	Youngsville	Terrebonne
Singer	Saline L.		Wildsville	Union
Sugartown	Sweet L.			Vermilion
Turkey Creek	Turkey Cr. L.			Vernon
Vixen	Vernon L.			W. Feliciana
Welcome	White L.			Winn

N
NW   NE
W   E
SW   SE
S

Puzzle solutions, pages 54-64

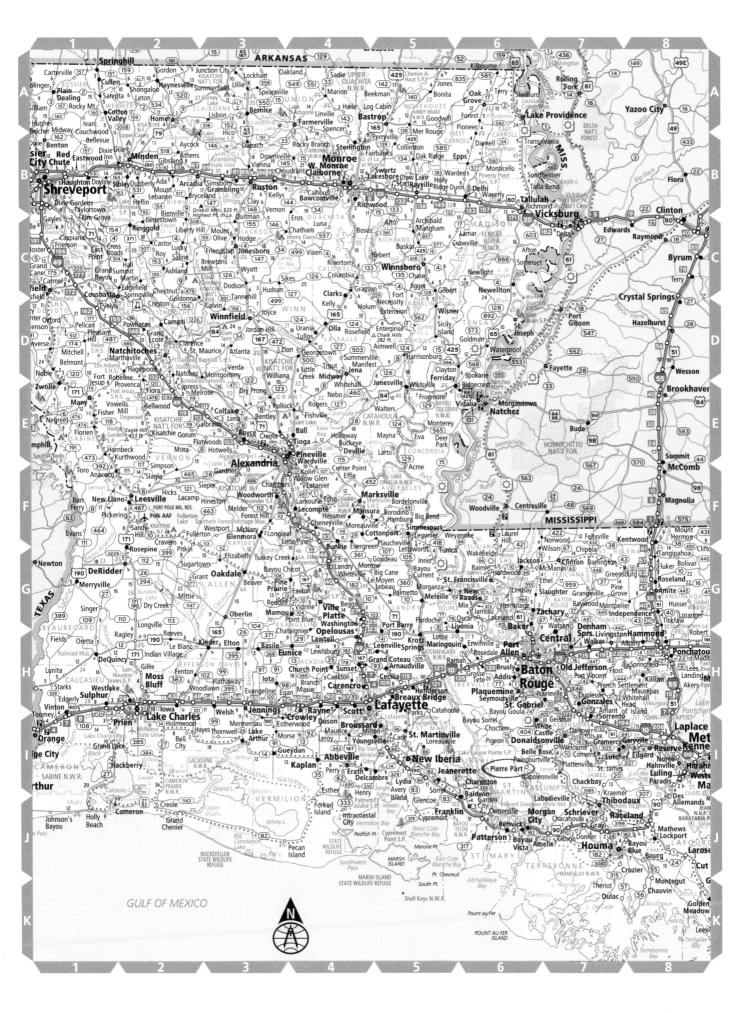

Maine The Pine Tree State

See Maine—see the world. Ok, that's not exactly true. More like worldly named Maine towns. In Lynchville stands the Maine World Traveler Sign that points you in the direction of nearby Denmark, Naples, China, Mexico, Peru, Poland and Paris, all just up the road apiece. Erected in the 1930s to promote tourism, the sign is still doing its job as a photo op and starting point for many Maine globetrotters.

In the northeasternmost state, adventure lies in every direction. Maine is the end of the Appalachian Trail; it has loads of moose; red-striped lighthouses; rocky coastlines; sandy beaches; mountains for hiking; a desert (yes!); and "lobstah" like nowhere else.

How to Map It!™ *Use the list below to seek a challenge found on the map. Once found, circle or highlight, then jot down the map coordinates next to the listed challenge to mark it as solved (see sample.) Coordinates can be found using the letter and number grids that frame the map.*

Towns	Towns-Stars & Stripes	Rivers & Creeks	Villes	Lakes & Ponds
Lynchville *G1*	Clinton	Big Wilson	Brooksville	Alligator L.
Athens	Freedom	Brassua	Brownville	Baker Pond
Belfast	Hancock	Carrabassett	Cardville	Duck Lake
China	Harmony	Dole	Chesterville	Echo L.
Denmark	Hope	Kennebago	Cornville	Great Moose L.
East Peru	Jackson	Kennebec	Greenville	Lobster Lake
Lebanon	Jefferson	Ossipee	Lincolnville	Moose Pd.
Lisbon	Liberty	Passadumkeag	Martinsville	Moosehead Lake
Madrid	Lincoln	Penobscot	Oceanville	Moxie Pond
Mexico	Madison	Pine	Sangerville	Pushaw
Moscow	Monroe	Saco	Stacyville	Rainbow Lake
Naples	Plymouth	Sebasticook	Swanville	Sheepscot Pond
Norway	Union	Sebec	Waterville	Spectacle Pond
Poland	Unity	St. George		Unity Pnd.
Rome	Washington	Union		
S. Paris		W. Br. Pleasant		
Vienna				

N
NW   NE
W   E
SW   SE
S

Puzzle solutions, pages 54-64

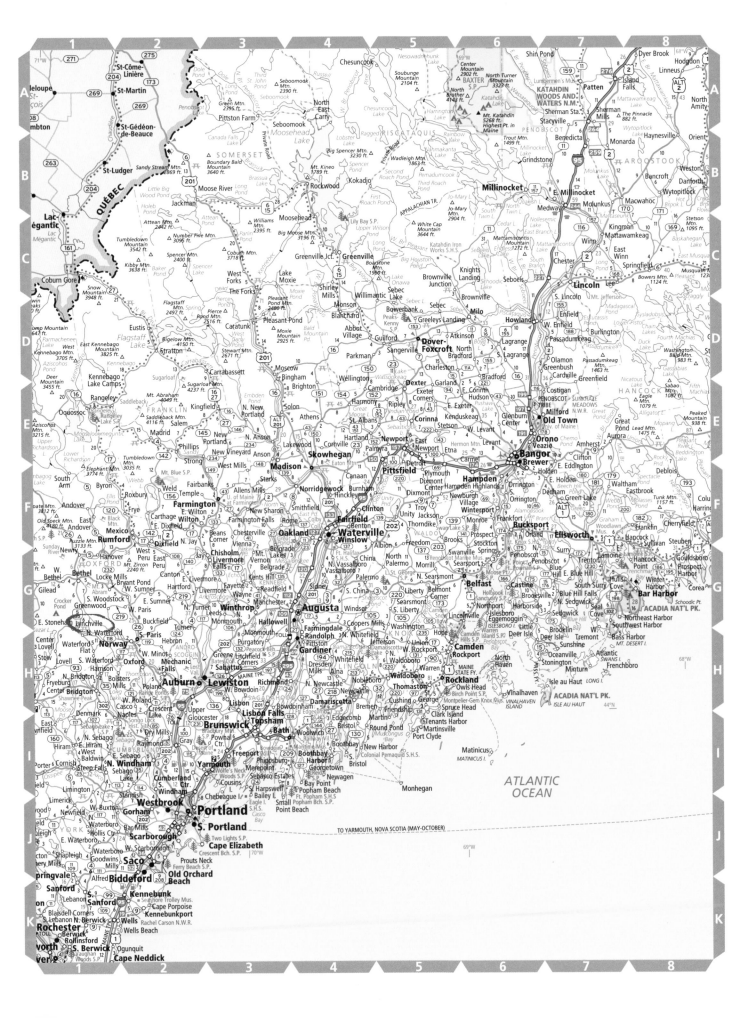

Maryland The Old Line State

Ever seen a bald eagle? What about lots of bald eagles, sometimes hundreds? Bring your camera to Maryland's Conowingo Dam on the Susquehanna River and that's what you'll find. At the dam, as the river's water level rises, many types of large fish will swim near the surface and the bald eagles swoop in for the day's catch. It is nature at its most majestic.

Don't miss Maryland's many other amazing places, like the Chesapeake Bay, Fort McHenry, birthplace of our national anthem, any crab shack serving Maryland blue crabs, and some of the oldest cities in America, all packed into this small state.

How to Map It!™ Use the list below to seek a challenge found on the map. Once found, circle or highlight, then jot down the map coordinates next to the listed challenge to mark it as solved (see sample.) Coordinates can be found using the letter and number grids that frame the map.

Towns

Bishops Head **J7**
Drybranch
Forest Hill
Friendship
Gratitude
Long Beach
Mount Harmony
Mount Pleasant
Roberts
Shiloh
Silver Spring
Starr
Still Pond
Sunshine
Uniontown
Welcome
Woodstock

Rivers & Creeks

Chester
Choptank
Deer
N. Br. Patapsco
Patuxent
Piscataway
Potomac*
Sams
Transquaking
Tuckahoe Cr.
Winters Run

Lakes

Big Elk
Liberty L.
Prettyboy Res.
Triadelphia Res.

State Parks & Rec

Calvert Cliffs
Cedarville S.F.
Elk Neck
Greenwell
Gunpowder Falls
Hart-Miller Island
Martinak
Merkle Wildlife Sanctuary
Patapsco Valley
Patuxent R.
Point Lookout
Rocks
Rosaryville
Seneca Creek
Smallwood
St. Mary's River
Susquehanna

Villes

Birdsville
Burrisville
Churchville
Cooksville
Dawsonville
Earleville
Ewingville
Hughesville
Johnsville
Loveville
Mechanicsville
Shawsville
Taylorsville
Unionville
Walkersville

Points

Breezy Point
Coltons Point
Cove Point
Drum Point
Hack Point
Piney Point
Rock Point

Counties

Baltimore
Carroll
Charles
Dorchester
Queen Anne's
Talbot

*Multiple coordinates

N
NW   NE
W   E
SW   SE
S

Puzzle solutions, pages 54-64

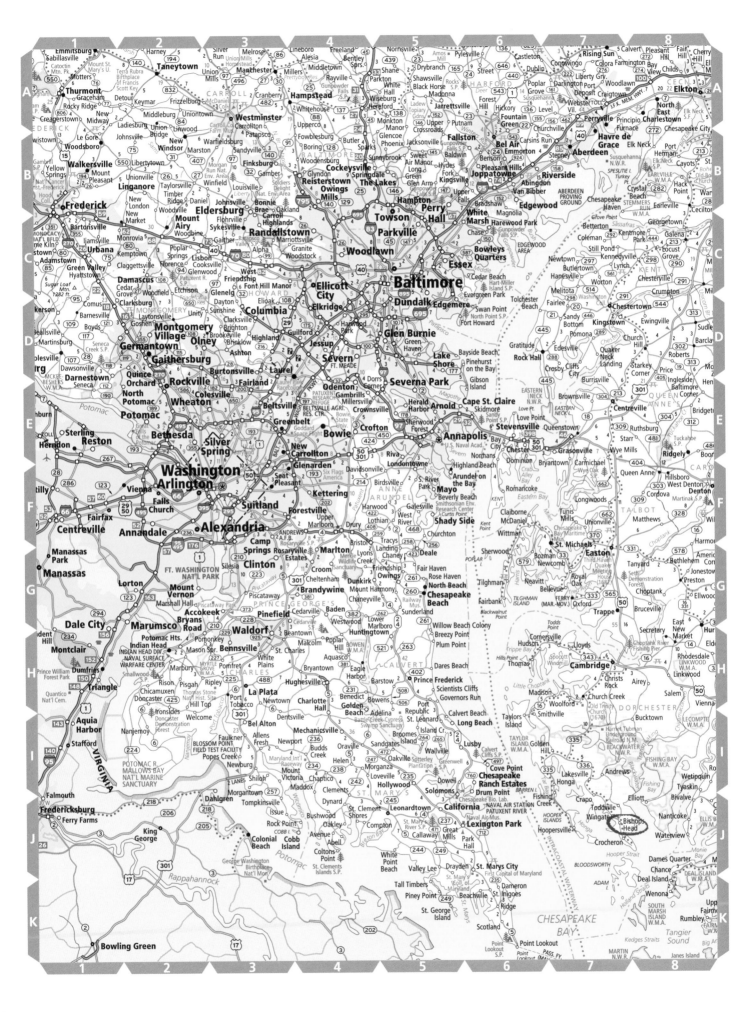

Massachusetts The Bay State

You've heard of Stonehenge. How about Ponyhenge? Not ancient but way more fun. In 2010, in a Lincoln, Massachusetts pasture, one rusty hobbyhorse appeared. No one admits to knowing how or why. But since, more horses—rocking, figurines, plastic ponies—have joined the herd. Some days they form a circle or a racing line. Mysteriously, they just keep turning up.

As for the rest of Massachusetts, The Plymouth Pilgrims, Boston's Freedom Trail, Cape Cod, state parks, New England towns, it's no mystery why this must-visit original colony is still an original.

How to Map It!™ Use the list below to seek a challenge found on the map. Once found, circle or highlight, then jot down the map coordinates next to the listed challenge to mark it as solved (see sample.) Coordinates can be found using the letter and number grids that frame the map.

Towns	Lakes	Villes	State Parks & Rec	Rivers & Creeks
Lincoln *C5*	Bare Hill Pd.	Barrowsville	Ashland	Charles*
Ashby	Buffumville L.	Bryantville	Borderland	Cole
Berlin	Burrage Pd.	Cordaville	Boxford	Concord
Dover	Chauncy L.	Fisherville	Callahan	Ipswich
Five Corners	Fort Meadow Res.	Hortonville	Cochituate	Mill
Georgetown	Hickory Hills L.	Lakeville	Demarest Lloyd	N. Nashua
Halifax	Knops Pd.	Rockville	Dighton Rock	Nashua
Lambs Grove	L. Shirley	Sheldonville	Dunn	Nemasket
Long Plain	L. Wampanoag	Waterville	Fort Phoenix St. Res.	Palmer
Middleborough	Lake Winthrop	Wellville	Great Broo Farm	Paskamanset
Nahant	Long Pd.	Wheelockville	Harold Parker S.F.	Quinapoxet
Nipmuck Pond	Mascuppic L.	Whitinsville	Leominster S.F.	Quinebaug
Norwell	Massapoag Lake		Massasoit	Squannacook
Pine Rest	Massapoag Pond	**Counties**	Pearl Hill	Three Mile
Princeton	Singletary Pd.	Bristol	Purgatory Chasm S.R.	Whitman
Silver Lake	Stiles Res.	Essex	Rutland	Winnetuxet
South Westport	Sudbury Res.	Middlesex	Spencer S.F.	
Still River	Sunset L.	Norfolk*	Waldon Pond S.R.	
Sutton		Suffolk	Willowdale S.F.	
Upton				

*Multiple coordinates

Puzzle solutions, pages 54-64

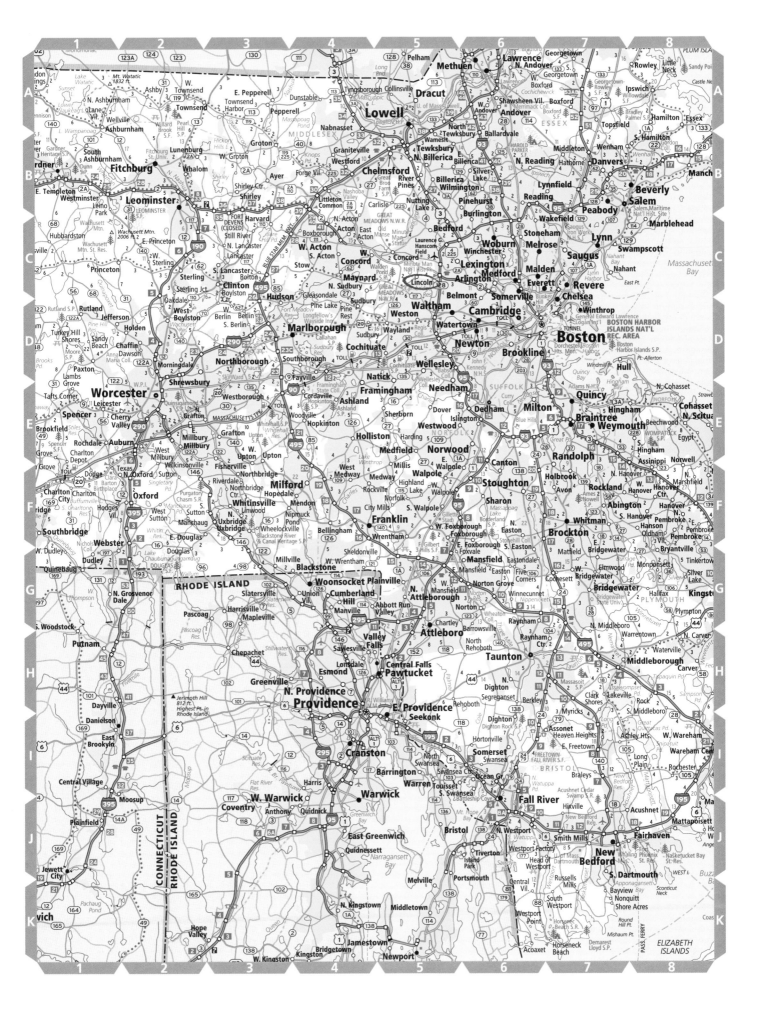

Michigan The Great Lake(s) State

A Michigan visit can be a helluva lot of fun—especially in Hell, MI. This small town makes the most of its name. You can send a fire-singed postcard stamped "Been through Hell" at the post office (located inside the Hell Hole Diner of course.) Then have some ice cream at the Creamatory and in winter you can see Hell freeze over.

Heck you even can be mayor of Hell for a day, an office from which you are promptly impeached at five p.m., but you get to keep the t-shirt.

Want more wholesome fun? Michigan's best feature is its lakes. Touching four Great Lakes and holding 11,000 inland lakes, spread across its upper and lower peninsulas, it is a water world full up on boating, skiing, huge sand dunes, wineries, big cities and charming towns for visits as great as its lakes.

How to *Map It!*™ Use the list below to seek a challenge found on the map. Once found, circle or highlight, then jot down the map coordinates next to the listed challenge to mark it as solved (see sample.) Coordinates can be found using the letter and number grids that frame the map.

Towns	Rivers & Creeks	Lakes	State Parks & Rec	Counties
Hell *I7*	Au Gres	Big Star L.	Bay City St. Rec. Area	Allegan
Azalia	Chippewa	Center L.	Brighton S.R.A.	Bay
Bell Oak	Dowagiac	Chippewa L.	Cambridge Jct. Hist.	Barry
Butternut	Flat	Crooked L.	Ft. Custer S.R.A.	Clare
Cascade	Flint*	Crystal L.	Highland S.R.A.	Gladwin
Delano	Grand*	Devils L.	Holly S.R.A.	Kalkaska
Easton	Gun	Green Lake	Interlochen	Ionia
Ferry	Little Manistee	Gun L.	Island Lake S.R.A.	Isabella
Hannah	Looking Glass	Houghton L.	Kal-Haven Tr.	Mecosta
Hope	Pine*	Indian L.	Rifle River S.R.A.	Missaukee
Lacey	Pentwater	L. Fenton	Sleepy Hollow	Oceana
Paris	Rabbit	L. St. Helen	Walter J. Hayes	Saginaw
Peacock	Rifle	Lincoln L.	William Mitchell	Van Buren
Ridgeway	Saline	Long L.*	Yankee Springs S.R.A.	Wexford
Shady Shores	Shiawassee*	Spider L..		
Tuscola	Thornapple	Wiggins L.		
Westphalia	Tobacco			

*Multiple coordinates

Puzzle solutions, pages 54-64

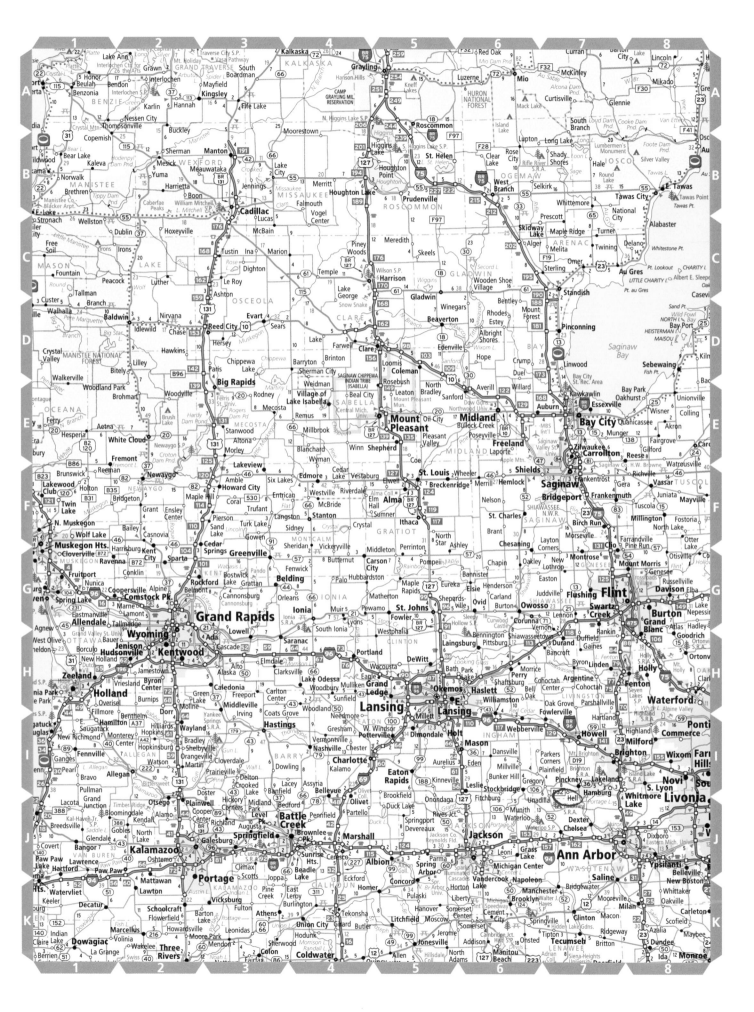

Minnesota Land of 10,000 Lakes

Ol' Man River keeps on rollin'…sure, but from where? Park Rapids, MN in Itasca State Park is where you'll find the Mississippi River headwaters. Just 18 feet across and inches deep, you can wade over to the other side. They say if you make a wish while crossing, it will come true by the time the water reaches the Gulf of Mexico 2,320 miles away.

Wish for more? Well, there's more Minnesota shoreline than CA, HI and FL combined. Water skiing and snowmobiling were invented here. There's great Twin Cities hiking trails and a 52-block Minneapolis skyway system so you can eat, live, and work warmly in winter.

How to *Map It!*™ *Use the list below to seek a challenge found on the map. Once found, circle or highlight, then jot down the map coordinates next to the listed challenge to mark it as solved (see sample.) Coordinates can be found using the letter and number grids that frame the map.*

His Town	Her Town	Rivers & Creeks	Villes	Lakes
Andree E8	Alberta	Beaver	Albertville	Buffalo L.
Brandon	Bertha	Buffalo Cr.	Brennyville	Eagle L.
Carlos	Clara City	Chippewa	Browerville	Fish Lake
Evan	Clarissa	Cottonwood	Collegeville	Fishhook L.
Fernando	Elizabeth	Crow Wing	Evansville	Fish Trap L.
Garrison	Emily	Little Rock	Georgeville	Goose Lake
Glen	Florence	Long Prairie	Huntersville	Gull Lake
Herman	Hadley	Minnesota*	Janesville	Loon Lake
Lincoln	Lydia	Otter Tail	Lakeville	North Turtle L.
Marty	Madison	Redeye	Millerville	Otter Tail Lake
Nelson	Nicollet	Rum	Paynesville	Pelican Lake
Ramsey	Olivia	Sauk*	Renville	Rabbit Lake
Raymond	Rose City	Shakopee	Richville	Skunk Lake
Russell	Stacy	Shell	Shieldsville	Swan Lake
Stewart	Tracy	Snake	Swanville	Toad L.
Tyler	Victoria	Yellow Medicine	Waterville	Wolf L.
Wendell	Wanda	Wing		

*Multiple coordinates

W   E

S

Puzzle solutions, pages 54-64

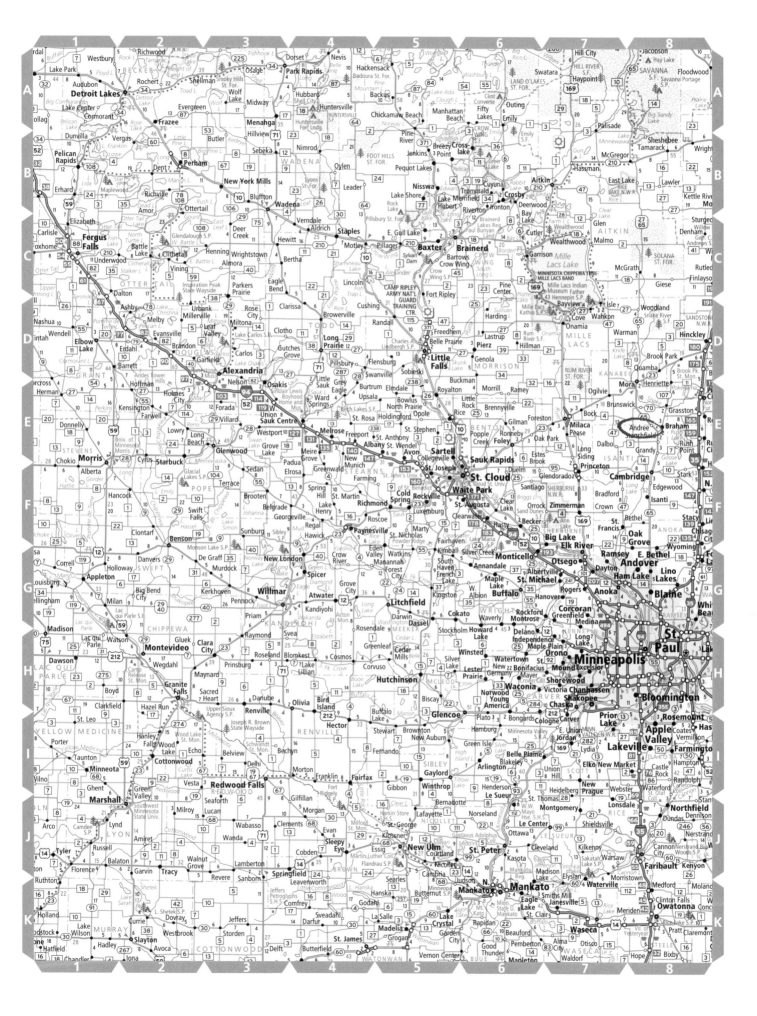

Mississippi The Magnolia State

Quick...where is Kermit the Frog from? Sesame Street? Wrong. He's from Leland, Mississippi. His creator Jim Henson went to school in Leland and spent time with a friend named Kermit exploring the froggy Mississippi Delta swamps. Now it is home to the Jim Henson Memorial and Muppet Museum where you can see an original Kermit playing his banjo in the Mississippi swamp, hug a giant Kermit and take in other Muppety sights. Best part? It's easy because it won't cost you any green.

It's not all frogs and swamps. The Delta is also the birthplace of the blues. Then there's the Mississippi beaches on the Gulf of Mexico, the river towns, Elvis's Tupelo home, the food (*mmm*), hiking, canoeing and the magnolias in bloom.

How to Map It!™ *Use the list below to seek a challenge found on the map. Once found, circle or highlight, then jot down the map coordinates next to the listed challenge to mark it as solved (see sample.) Coordinates can be found using the letter and number grids that frame the map.*

Towns

Leland *E2*
Alcorn
Black Hawk
Bourbon
Duck Hill
Falcon
Good Hope
Hot Coffee
Hurricane
Kokomo
Laws Hill
Moscow
Peoples
Pope
Rome
Tallula
Thrashers
Whites
Yazoo City

*Multiple coordinates

Rivers & Creeks

Bayou Pierre
Big Sunflower
Bowie Cr.
Buckatunna Cr.
Chiwapa
Chunky
Coldwater
Deer Cr.
Homochitto
Leaf
Line Cr.
Pearl
Skuna
Strong
Tippah
Tombigbee
W. Tallahala
Yazoo*
Yockanookany

Lakes

Aberdeen Lake
Arkabutla L.
Bay Springs L.
Bluff L.
Eagle Lake
Enid Lake
Flower L.
Grenada L.
Lake Bogue Homo
Lake Bolivar
Moon Lake
Okatibbee Lake
Sardis Lake

State Parks & Rec

Florewood
Great River Road

Hugh White
John W. Kyle
Natchez
Percy Quin
Tombigbee
Trace
Wall Doxey

Villes

Brooksville
Brownsville
Coffeeville
Doddsville
Evansville
Forkville
Garlandville
Gatesville
Geeville
Hermanville
Knoxville

Leaksville
Louisville
Mayersville
Springville
Taylorsville
Woodville

Counties

Adams
Copiah
Franklin
Greene
Holmes
Itawamba
Jasper
Leake
Marshall
Pontotoc
Sunflower
Tallahatchie

N
W E
S

Puzzle solutions, pages 54-64

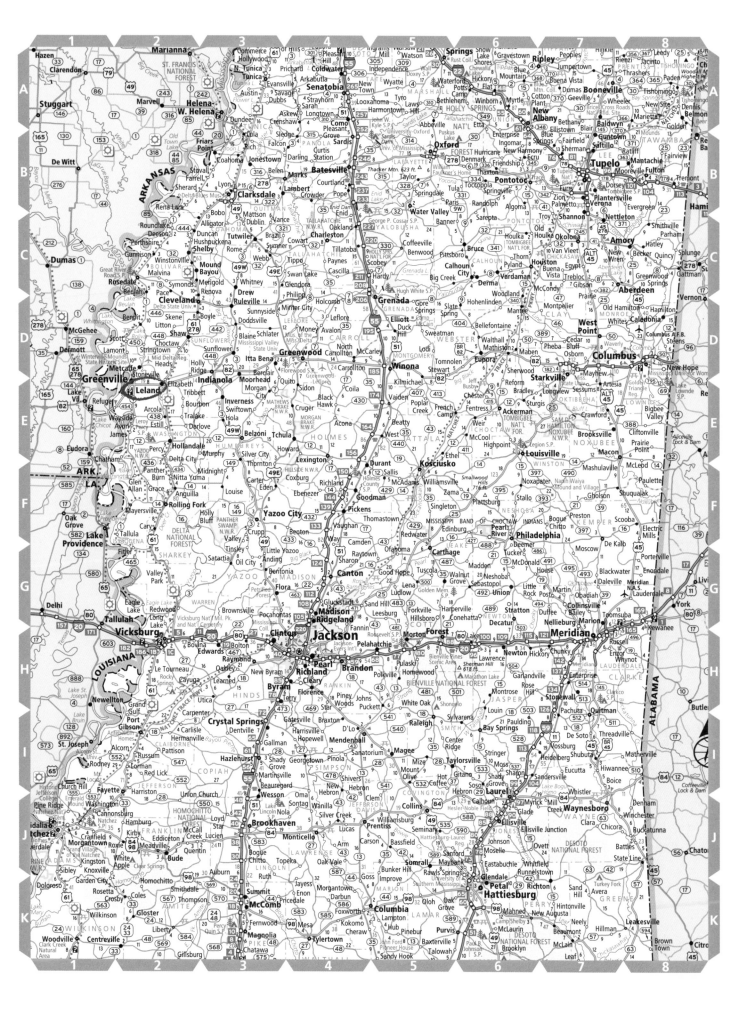

Missouri The Show-Me State

Remember U.S. President David Rice Atchison of Plattsburg, MO? No? Maybe that's because he was only president for a day. On Sunday, March 4, 1849 James Polk left office, but president-elect Zachary Taylor and his VP refused to be sworn in on the Sabbath. So Atchison, President of the Senate that day, became acting VP, and therefore president. Atchison said his was "the honestest administration this country ever had." His Plattsburg grave declares him president for one day. All true.

Missouri has other surprises like the Ozark Mountains and lakes, Kansas City BBQ, caves to spelunk, rivers to float and fish, and rocks to climb. Show me!

How to *Map It!*™ Use the list below to seek a challenge found on the map. Once found, circle or highlight, then jot down the map coordinates next to the listed challenge to mark it as solved (see sample.) Coordinates can be found using the letter and number grids that frame the map.

Towns	Rivers & Creeks	Lakes	Counties	Villes
Plattsburg **B1**	Beaver Cr.	Lake of the Ozarks	Barry	Abesville
Amsterdam	Blackwater	Long Branch L.	Cedar	Bradleyville
Bearcreek	Bourbeuse	Mark Twain L.	Cole	Curryville
Camden	Crooked	Pomme de Terre L.	Cooper	Darksville
Competition	Eleven Point	Silver Lake	Dade	Etterville
Couch	Gasconade*	Smithville L.	Daviess	Farmersville
Deepwater	Grand	Stockton Res.	Hickory	Gainesville
Dora	Horse Cr.	Swan Lake	Jackson	Hartville
Farmer	Jacks Fork		Jasper	Humansville
Glasgow	Lamine	**State Parks & Rec**	Marion	Kingsville
Grayson	Little Niangua	Arrow Rock S.H.S.	Osage	Marionville
Henley	Meramec	Bennett Spring	Phelps	Moundville
Japan	Missouri*	Big Sugar Cr.	Ray	Nashville
Kidder	N. Fork Salt	Finger Lakes	Stone	Otterville
Milo	S. Grand	Graham Cave	Texas	Pineville
Polo	S. Fabius	Ha Ha Tonka	Vernon	Pottersville
Prairie Hill	Salt	Harry S. Truman		Rockville
Santa Fe	Spring	Katy Trail*		Summersville
Stony Hill		Knob Noster		Taneyville
Union City		Long Br.		Windyville

*Multiple coordinates

Puzzle solutions, pages 54-64

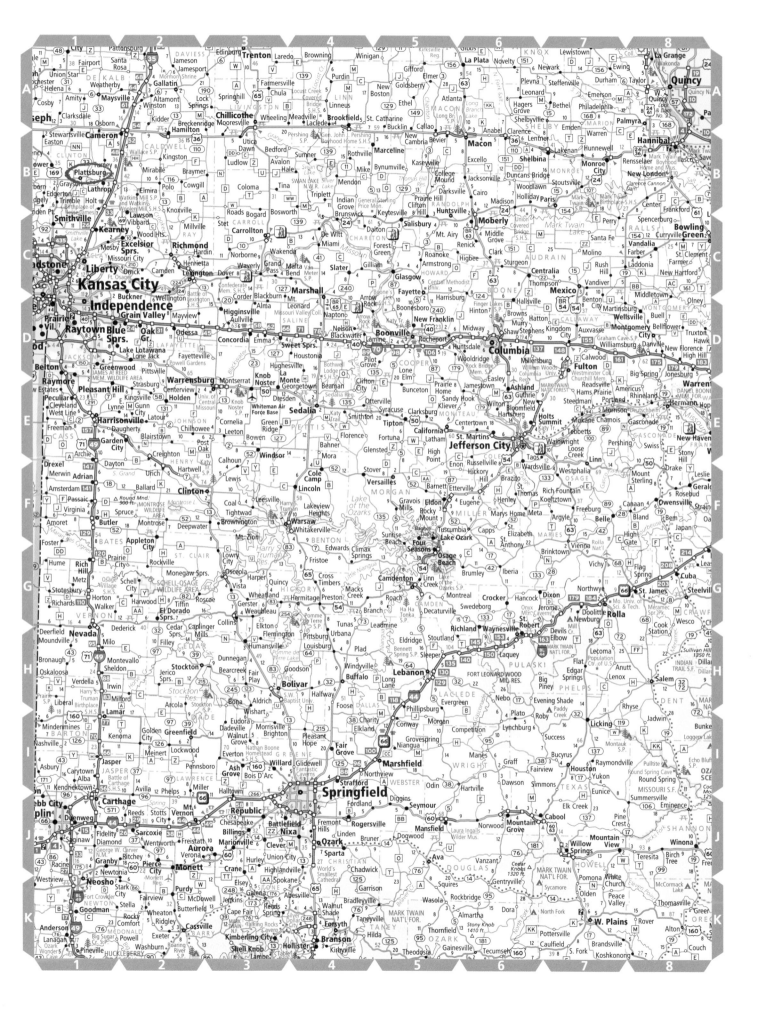

Montana The Treasure State

Glacier National Park, Montana is all picturesque vistas. But if you're on one side of the Ptarmigan Wall, a mountain from where the scenery is some of Glacier's best, you may have major "fomo" (fear of missing out) for the view on the other side. Lucky for you, in 1930 before "fomo" was a thing, the Civilian Conservation Corp. forged the Ptarmigan Tunnel to allow for the added view. Using jackhammers and dynamite they forced a 200-foot long tunnel through the rock. Now you can walk right through the mountain to see what you fear you're missing.

Like Glacier, you see beauty in every direction in Montana Big Sky Country. Split by the Continental Divide, on the west side of the state are Rocky Mountain ranges on the east side is Yellowstone National Park, Great Plains and badlands. Go. Don't miss out.

How to Map It!™ Use the list below to seek a challenge found on the map. Once found, circle or highlight, then jot down the map coordinates next to the listed challenge to mark it as solved (see sample.) Coordinates can be found using the letter and number grids that frame the map.

Towns	Rivers & Creeks	Lakes	State Parks & Rec	Counties
Augusta D3	Beaverhead	Big Salmon L.	Ackley Lake	Broadwater
Brady	Belt Cr.	Canyon Ferry Lake	Anaconda Smoke Stack	Cascade
Buffalo	Birch Cr.	Cataract Lake	Bannack	Chouteau
Checkerboard	Bitterroot	Ennis Lake	Beavertail Hill	Deer Lodge
Condon	Blackfoot	Freezeout Lake	Black Sandy	Flathead
Elliston	Boulder*	Harwood Lake	Elkhorn	Glacier
Essex	Cut Bank Cr.	Hay Lake	First Peoples Buffalo Jump	Granite
Harrison	Dearborn	Holter Lake	Giant Springs	Hill
Jackson	Grasshopper Cr.	Lake Agnes	Greycliff Prairie Dog Town	Jefferson
McLeod	Milk*	Lake Elwell	Lost Cr.	Lewis and Clark
Melville	Nevada Cr.	Lonesome Lake	Missouri Headwaters	Madison
Moore	Rossfork Cr.	Lower Glaston Lake	Parker Homestead	Meagher
Ovando	Ruby	Lower St. Mary Lake	Placid Lake	Park
Pine Creek	Sage Cr.	Mission Lake	Salmon Lake	Pondera
Pony	Stillwater	Placid Lake	Spring Meadow Lake	Silver Bow
Sun River	Sun	Salmon Lake	Tower Rock	Sweet Grass
Willow Creek	Sweet Grass Cr.	Swan Lake		Toole
Wisdom	Wise			Wheatland

*Multiple coordinates

W · E
S

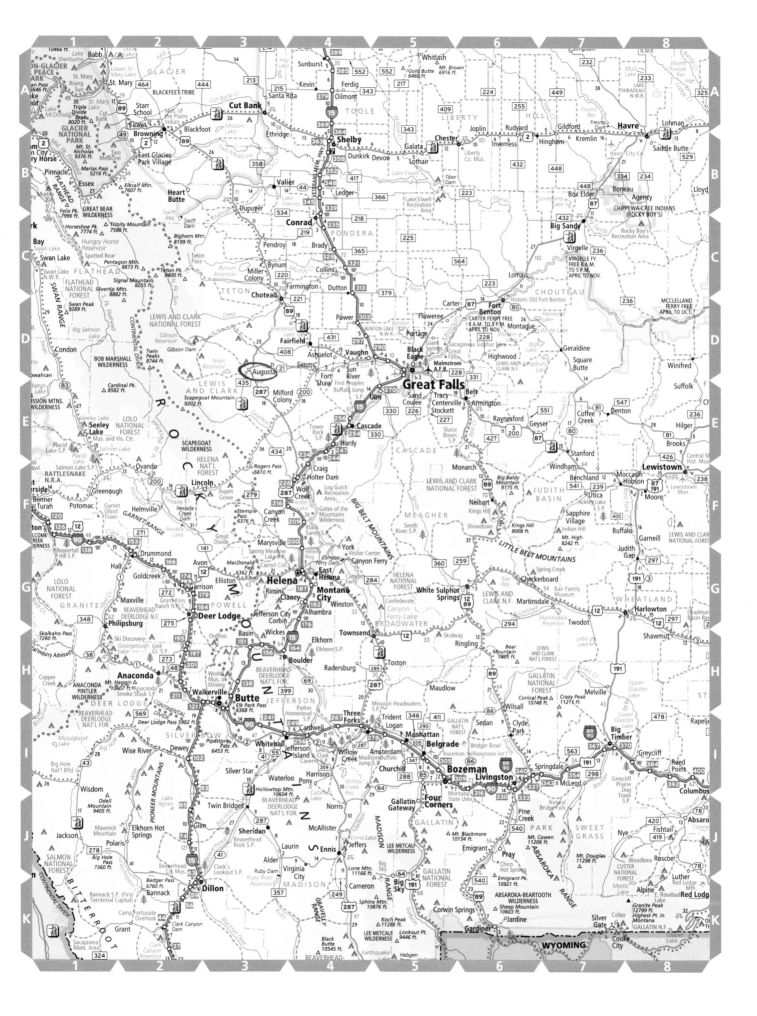

Nebraska The Cornhusker State

Lewis and Clark explored Nebraska in canoes. You can do it by tank. Not the army kind, but the big, surprisingly buoyant, livestock-grain-tank-kind that float on the Cedar River through Fullerton, Spalding and Ericson, NE. Tanking is the combination of two Nebraska resources—slow moving rivers and farm equipment. You and your friends relax inside the tank, some with built-in tables and benches, and go with the flow. Enjoy the scenery, the local otters and eagles, eat, drink—all from inside a tank from where cows used to eat.

Step outside your tank and you'll find Nebraska's got Great Plains prairies, massive Sand Hill dunes, breath-taking rock formations, and pioneer life that encompasses Native American history, to early American explorers to the space race.

How to *Map It!*™ Use the list below to seek a challenge found on the map. Once found, circle or highlight, then jot down the map coordinates next to the listed challenge to mark it as solved (see sample.) Coordinates can be found using the letter and number grids that frame the map.

Towns

Ericson **E5**
Ashton
Beaver City
Blue Hill
Bruning
Burton
Dunning
Friend
Fullerton
Holbrook
Long Pine
Lushton
Oconto
Oxford
Poole
Republican City
Sargent
Scotia
Spalding
Sumner
Worms

Villes

Eddyville
Hordville
Raeville
Rockville
Saronville
Westerville
Wilsonville

State Parks & Rec

Atkinson Lake S.R.A.
Bowman Lake St.
 Rec. Area
Calamus St. Rec. Area
Cheyenne S.R.A.
Fort Kearny St. Hist. Pk.
Lewis & Clark S.R.A.
Long Lake St. Rec. Area
Long Pine St. Rec. Area
Mormon I. S.R.A.
Niobrara
North Loup S.R.A.
Smith Falls
Victoria Springs St.
 Rec. Area
Willow Creek St.
 Rec. Area

Lakes

Calamus Reservoir
Elwood Res.
Johnson Res.
Lewis & Clark Lake
Moon Lake
Sherman Reservoir

Rivers & Creeks

Beaver Cr.
Big Blue
Calamus
Cedar
Medicine Cr.
Middle Loup
Niobrara
Platte
South Fork Elkhorn

Counties

Antelope
Blaine
Boone
Boyd
Brown
Dawson
Fillmore
Garfield
Greeley
Hall
Hamilton
Holt
Knox
Loup
Phelps
Rock
Thayer
Valley
Wheeler

N
NW
NE
W
E
SW
SE
S

Puzzle solutions, pages 54-64

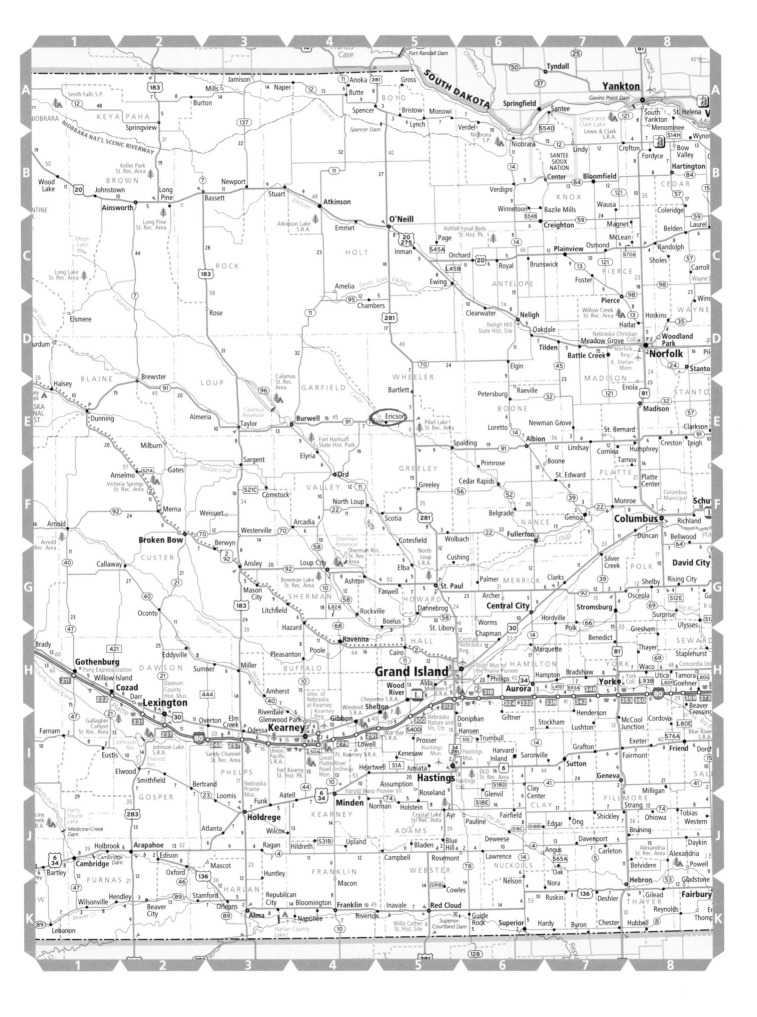

Alabama

Towns
C6 Oak Grove
D7 Alexander City
A3 America
B8 Barfield
C1 Buhl
J3 Burnt Corn
B6 Calcis
I3 Chestnut
A2 Corona
E5 Fairview
F7 Friendship
A3 Gorgas
D2 Havana
B7 Jenifer
E4 Lawley
C4 Marvel
D7 Mount Olive
A4 Mt. Olive
B6 New London
K5 Paul
H7 Pine Level
H8 Omega
H7 Orion
I1 Salitpa
D4 Six Mile
H4 Snow Hill
E8 Thornton
D6 Unity
B7 Waldo
A8 White Plains

Rivers & Creeks
K3 Big Escambia Cr.
E1 Black Warrior
H4 Cedar Cr.
C6 Coosa
K2 Little R.
E4 Mulberry Cr.
K7 Pea River
J5 Pigeon Cr.
G6 Pintlala Cr.
J4 Sepulga
C1 Sipsey River
J1 Tombigbee

Lakes
B3 Bankhead L.
I7 Conecuh
K6 Gantt L.
F6 Jordon Lake
D6 L. Mitchell
C2 L. Tuscaloosa

F1 Lake Demopolis
J8 Lake Tholocco
D6 Lay Lake
B6 Logan Martin L.
E8 Martin Lake

Villes
B4 Adamsville
J3 Belleville
C4 Brantleyville
K4 Centerville
J7 Clintonville
G8 Davisville
F6 Deatsville
I8 Elamville
H4 Farmersville
D8 Goldville
G5 Gordonsville
F6 Holtville
K4 Johnstonville
C8 Lineville
E4 Maplesville
C7 Millerville
B1 Newtonville
B6, E4 Plantersville
J2 Suggsville
J1 Wagarville

Counties
D4 Bibb
I1 Clarke
J7 Coffee
J4 Conecuh
K6 Covington
F3 Dallas
K3 Escambia
A2 Fayette
D1 Greene
E2 Hale
B3 Jefferson
G5 Lowndes
G8 Macon
G2 Marengo
F3 Perry
I8 Pike
A7 St. Clair
B7 Talladega
E8 Tallapoosa

Arizona

Towns
K1 Why
D3 Cherry
K3 Comobabi
K7 Dragoon
F7 Fort Apache
J4 Friendly Corners
H7 Geronimo
E8 Indian Pine
D1 Kirkland
I4 La Palma
I4 Picacho
F4 Punkin Center
J5 Rillito
E3 Rock Springs
D4 Strawberry
I1 Theba
G4 Tortilla Flat
J8 Turkey Flat
A3 Valle
E5 Young

Rivers & Creeks
E3 Agua Fria
I6 Aravaipa Cr.
F8 Big Bonito Cr.
B1 Big Chino Wash
F6 Canyon Cr.
E5 Cherry Cr.
C6 Clear Cr.
C5 Cottonwood Wash
H1, H4 Gila
E1 Hassayampa
A4, D8 Little Colorado
F8 N. Fk. White
I1 Quilotosa Wash.
F6 Salt
G7 San Carlos
K7 San Pedro
E5 Tonto Cr.
F7 White

Lakes
G4 Apache L.
F4 Bartlett Res.
D5 Blue Ridge Res.
D5 Chevelon Canyon L.
E3 Horseshoe Res.
F2 L. Pleasant
C4 Mormon L.
H7 San Carlos Res.
F5 Theodore Roosevelt Lake

Counties
K8 Cochise
F1 Maricopa
A7 Navajo
K4 Pima
C1 Yavapai

State Parks & Rec
H5 Boyce Thompson Arboretum
J5 Catalina
C3 Dead Horse Ranch
E7 Fool Hollow Lake Rec. Area
D3 Ft. Verde St. Hist. Pk.
E1 Granite Mtn. Hotshots Memorial
B6 Homolovi
G4 Lost Dutchman
H4 McFarland St. Hist. Pk.
J6 Oracle
J4 Picacho Peak
C3 Red Rock
I8 Roper Lake
C3 Slide Rock
D4 Tonto Natural Bridge

Camp Sites
D5 Blue Ridge
D5 Chevelon Lake
E5 Christopher Cr.
C4 Dairy Springs
D2 Granite Basin
B2 Kaibab Lake
C4 Kinnikinick Lake
E8 Lakeside
C4 Manzanita
B4 Pinegrove
E5 Ponderosa
D5 Rock Crossing
J6 Rose Canyon
I8 Soldier Creek
J6 Spencer Canyon
G4 Tortilla
D2 White Spar
D2 Wolf Cr.

Arkansas

Towns
F1 Big Fork
C4 Blackwell
B1 Cecil
I2 Columbus
B8 Floral
B5 Formosa
B2 Harmony
C4 Hattieville
I5 Holly Springs
H7 Ladd
K4 Lisbon
H3 Okolona
I2 Perrytown
C8 Providence
I1 Saratoga
C5 St. Vincent
H5 Tulid
I8 Tyro
F7 Wright
H8 Yorktown

Rivers & Creeks
B2 Arkansas
H8 Bayou Bartholomew
D8 Bayou des Arc
B3 Big Piney Cr.
C5 Cadron
J8 Cutoff
D4 Fourche LaFave
H2 Little Missouri
B8 Little Red
I6 Moro Cr.
F1 Ouachita
D2 Petite Jean
K1 Red
H6 Saline
B5 S. Fk. Little Red
K4 Smackover Cr.

Lakes
D2 Blue Mountain L.
B3 Dardanelle L.
G3 Degray L.
D6 L. Conway
K2 L. Erling
G1 L. Greeson
E5 L. Maumelle
F3 L. Ouachita
E4 L. Winona
B7 Little Red
I1 Millwood L.
B1 Ozark L.
E8 Peckerwood L.
I4 White Oak L.

State Parks & Rec
I8 Cane Cr.
H2 Crater of Diamonds
G2 Daisy
I2 Historic Washington
G5 Jenkins Ferry
G4 Lake Catherine
C3 Lake Dardanelle
F3 Lake Ouachita
K3 Logoly
D8 Lower White River Mus.
I6 Marks' Mill
K6 Moro Bay
C2 Mt. Magazine
C3 Mt. Nebo
D4 Petite Jean
E5 Pinnacle Mtn.
E7 Plantation Agri. Mus.
J4 Poison Spr.
F6 Toltec Mnds. Archeological
I3 White Oak Lake
C6 Woolly Hollow

Counties
K8 Ashley
H4 Clark
J8 Drew
B1 Franklin
E3 Garland
G6 Grant
I2 Hempstead
G4 Hot Springs
G6 Jeffson
K2 Lafayette
E7 Lonoke
K1 Miller
D4 Perry
G2 Pike
B4 Pope
F7 Pulasky
E5 Saline
E1 Scott
D2 Yell

California

Towns
E1 Fort Bragg
C7 Caribou
K7 Crows Landing
H7 Drytown
B1 Eel Rock
F8 Gold Run
F2 Hopland
G5 Knights Landing
E1 Navarro
H2 Occidental
E7 Rough & Ready
I8 Sheep Ranch
H3 Tomales
A6 Viola
I7 Waterloo
G5 Yolo
B1 Zenia

Villes
F1 Boonville
A1 Bridgeville
I5 Collinsville
B5 Dairyville
H2 Forestville
E8 Graniteville
G3 Geyserville
B8 Janesville
F3 Kelseyville
D1 Laytonville
A4 Millville
H4 Oakville
G8 Placerville
G6 Roseville
F6 Smartville
C8 Taylorsville

Lakes
F6 Bear
C4 Black Butte Lake
C7 Bucks L.
I7 Camanche Res.
F3 Clear L.
A8 Eagle Lake
H4 L. Berryessa
C8 L. Davis
E3 L. Pillsbury
G2 L. Sonoma
B7 Lake Almanor
D6 Lake Oroville
J8 Modesto Res.
J8 New Melones L.
I7 Pardee Res.
K8 Turlock L.

Valleys
E6 Browns Valley
J4 Castro Valley
G7 Garden Valley
E7 Grass Valley
G7 Hidden Valley
C7 Meadow Valley
J3 Mill Valley
F7 Penn Valley
G4 Pope Valley
E2 Potter Valley
E2 Redwood Valley
D7 Stawberry Valley
H2 Valley Ford
J7 Valley Home
I8 Valley Springs

Rivers & Creeks
D2 Black Butte
C6, D5 Butte Cr.
G4 Cache Cr.
I7 Calaveras
C5 Deer Cr.
I7 Dry Cr.
D2, C1 Eel
F2 Garcia
A2 Hayfork Cr.
J7 Littlejohns Cr.
A1 Mad
A7 Pine Cr.
F8 Rubicon
G8 Silver Cr.
A1 Trinity
F6 Yuba

Colorado

Towns

H6 Cañon City
J6 Beulah
I8 Boone
B6 Campion
A2 Coalmont
C5 Eldora
D3 Gilman
G6 Goldfield
A4 Gould
C3 Heeney
B6 Hygiene
E4 Jefferson
J3 La Garita
E6 Louviers
A1 Milner
B6 Niwot
H2 Ohio
I1 Powderhorn
K5 Redwing
C4 Tabernash
G2 Tin Cup
D7 Watkins
H3 Whitepine

Rivers & Creeks

A5 Big Thompson
C3 Blue
B7 Box Elder Cr.
C2 Colorado
J7 Cucharas
E3 Eagle
C4 Fraser
E1 Fryingpan
J5 Grape Cr.
J7 Huerfano
A3 Illinois
E8 Kiowa Cr.
K1 Rio Grande
J3 Saguache Cr.
I4 San Luis Cr.
F5 S. Platte
J7 St. Charles
F5 Tarryall Cr.
G1 Taylor
H2 Tomichi Cr.
B4 Willow

Ski

D2 Beaver Cr.
F1 Buttermilk
C5 Eldora Mtn.
C4 Granby Ranch
A2 Howelsen Hill
D4 Loveland
H3 Monarch Mtn.
E3 Ski Cooper

Counties

K4 Alamosa
C5 Boulder
H3 Chaffee
D5 Clear Creek
D2 Eagle
G1 Gunnison
K6 Huerfano
K1 Mineral
F4 Park
K2 Rio Grande
J2 Saguache
G6 Teller

State Parks & Rec

C7 Barr Lake
A6 Boyd Lake
E6 Chatfield
C6 Eldorado Canyon
F5 Eleven Mile
C5 Golden Gate Canyon
I7 Lake Pueblo
K7 Lathrop
A6 Lory
G5 Mueller
K4 San Luis
B2 Stagecoach
A4 State Forest
E5 Staunton
B6 St. Vrain
D2 Sylvan Lake

Connecticut

Towns

H4 New Haven
C8 Coventry
H2 Easton
A5 Ebbs Corner
B6 East Granby
B5 Firetown
F3 Good Hill
A4 Hartland
H2 Long Hill
E7 Marlborough
F3 Oxford
H1 Redding
D1 South Kent
I2 Southport
C5 West Avon
C2 West Goshen
E4 Woodtick

Rivers & Creeks

H1 Aspetuck
D2 Bantam
A2 Blackberry
B4 Cherry Brook
F6 Coginchaug
G8 Connecticut
G5 Farm
C4 Farmington
G6 Hammonasset
C1, H3 Housantonic
B3, E4 Mad
F4 Mill
E6 Mattabesset
H2 Pequonnock
G1 Saugatuck
A6 Stony
B8 Willimantic

Lakes

E8 Amston L.
D8 Andover L.
C8 Bolton L.
F5 Broad Brook Res.
H2 Easton Res.
D4 Hancock Brook L.
G5 L. Gaillard
D1 L. Waramaug
C4 Nepaug Res.
D4 Old Marsh Pond
F8 Pickerel L.
E7 Pocotopaug L.
E3 L. Quassapaug

E4 Scoville Res.
E5 Silver L.
H3 Trap Falls Res.
A1 Twin Lakes
C8 Wangumbaug L.

Villes

A1 Amesville
C3 Bakersville
H1 Branchville
C4 Collinsville
E2 Hotchkissville
A7 Hazardville
F7 Leesville
F4 Mixville
E1 Northville
E4 Plantsville
C8 Quarryville
A7 Somersville
C4 Unionville
D4 Whigville

State Parks & Rec

B4 American Legion
B3 Burr Pond
E7 Dart Island
D6 Dinosaur
F3 Kettletown
D7 Gay City
B1 Housatonic Meadows
G3 Indian Well
E7 Meshomasic
B5 Penwood
G1 Putnam Mem.
A7 Scantic River
G8 Selden Neck
I3 Silver Sands
I2 Sherwood Island
G5 Wharton Brook

Florida

Towns

G2 Bayport
G8 Bellwood
G7 Christmas
C6 Crescent Beach
K6 De Soto City
E6 Emporia
E3 Fellowship
K8 Fort Drum
J6 Frostproof
I4 Keysville
D6 Lake Como
F5 Lisbon
H7 Narcoossee
C5 Orange Mills
F4 Oxford
I2 Ozona
D7 Painters Hill
C7 Summer Haven
C4 Waldo
G3 Weeki Wachee
E2 Yankeetown

Rivers & Creeks

H4 Hillsborough
K7 Kissimmee
K4 Manatee
B3 Olustee Cr.
K5 Peace
B2 Santa Fe

Lakes

H7 Alligator L.
J8 Blue Cypress Lake
K6 Lake June in Winter
J6 Crooked L.
B4 Kingsley Lake
D6 L. Disston
F5 L. Harris
H7 L. Hart
H8 L. Poinsett
I6 L. Rosalie
B4 L. Sampson
E3 L. Stafford
I2 L. Tarpon
F5 L. Yale
I8 Lake Hellen Blazes
K7 Lake Istokpoga
J7 Lake Marian
I6 Lake Marion
E3 Lake Rousseau
H8 Lake Winder
D3 Levy Lake
D4 Orange L.

F7 Puzzle Lake
C4 Santa Fe L.
F3 Tsala Apopka Lake

State Parks & Rec

F6 Blue Spr.
D7 Bulow Creek
I2 Caladesi Island
E2 Cedar Key Mus.
F2 Chrystal River Arch
H4 Colt Creek
F3 Ft. Cooper
G4 Dade Bfld. Hist
E6 De Leon Sprs.
D2 Fanning Springs
C7 Faver-Dykes
A2 Folk Culture Ctr.
B6 Guana River
K6 Highlands Hammock
F5 Lake Griffin
G5 Lake Louisa
K3 Lake Manatee
J6 Lake Wales Ridge
B1 Peacock Springs
E3 Rainbow Springs
C5 Ravine Gdns
D7 Tomoka
G3 Weeki Wachee Springs
G6 Wekiwa Sprs.
F3, G4 Withlacoochee S.F.

Counties

C3 Alachua
F3 Citrus
B5 Clay
A3 Columbia
A5 Duval
C2 Gilchrist
J4 Hillsborough
H5 Lake
K3 Manatee
E4 Marion
H7 Orange
I7 Osceola
H3 Pasco
I2 Pinellas
G7 Seminol
B6 St. Johns
F4 Sumter
B2 Suwannee
B3 Union

Georgia

Towns

G7 Adrian
B2 Austell
D8 Boneville
K5 Brookfield
H2 Brooklyn
H4 Dooling
A7 Fortsonia
B4 Good Hope
H4 Lilly
F4 Lizella
I8 Pine Grove
G3 Potterville
E4 Round Oak
F3 Salem
C1 Sand Hill
D4 Stewart
E3 The Rock
K7 Upton
B4 Youth
A6 Vanna

Rivers & Creeks

J4 Abrams
J8 Big Satilla
A6 Broad
E2 Flint
G6 Gum Swamp
I2 Kinchafoonee Cr.
F7 Little Ohoopee
I3 Muckalee Cr.
I6 Ocmulgee
I1 Pataula Cr.
K7 Satilla
C3 South
K1 Spring
G1 Upatoi
C4 Yellow

Villes

I5 Abbeville
D4 Adgateville
D8 Boneville
H4 Byromville
I8 Charlotteville
F6 Danville
H2 Draneville
H2 Ellaville
E2 Hollonville
J5 Irwinville
D1 Luthersville
E2 Meansville
A7 Ruckersville
I3 Smithville

J7 Snipesville
C4 Starrsville
B5 Watkinsville

State Parks & Rec

B7 Bobby Brown S.R.A.
F1 F.D.R.
J7 General Coffee
I4 Georgia Vet. Mem.
D7 Hamburg
D3 High Falls
D4 Indian Sprs.
K1 Kolomoki Mnds.
H7 Little Ocmulgee
C8 Mistletoe
C3 Panola Mtn.
A2 Red Top Mtn.
A7 Richard B. Russell
B2 Sweetwater Cr.
B6 Watson Mill Br.
B4 Will-A-Way S.R.A.

Counties

J8 Bacon
A4 Barrow
I5 Ben Hill
F4 Bibb
C1 Carroll
J1 Clay
C3 Clayton
B2 Cobb
C3 De Kalb
I4 Dooly
E3 Lamar
B8 Lincoln
E2 Meriwether
B5 Oconee
G4 Peach
E2 Pike
C3 Rockdale
K5 Tift
G8 Treutlen

Idaho

Towns

J4 Bliss
H2 Boise
I8 Bone
H6 Butte City
E5 Cobalt
G2 Crouch
J5 Eden
D3 Golden
A2 St. Joe
J3 King Hill
D2 Lucile
I5 Magic City
H7 Mud Lake
A1 Princeton
K8 Swanlake
H8 Thornton
C1 Waha

Rivers & Creeks

K2 Battle Cr.
H5, I6 Big Lost
G7 Birch Creek
J1 Castle Cr.
K5 Goose Cr.
K3 Jarbridge
B4 Kelly
C2 Lawyer
H6 Little Lost
F4 Loon
D3 Meadow Cr.
G7 Medicine Lodge
K1 Owyhee
E5 Panther Cr.
I1 Reynolds
C3 Selway
C1, F1 Snake

Lakes

H2 Arrowrock Res.
J8 Blackfoot Res.
K4 Cedar Creek Res.
G3 Deadwood Res.
E1 Hells Canyon Res.
F2 Lake Cascade
H7 Mud L.
G1 Paddock Valley Res.
F2 Payette L.
I8 Ririe Res.

Ski

E2 Brundage Mtn.
F2 Little Ski Hill
K6 Pomerelle Mtn.

H4 Soldier Mountian
H5 Sun Valley

State Parks & Rec

J3 Bruneau Dunes
I6 Craters of the Moon Nat'l Mon. and Preserve
B2 Dworshak
H2 Eagle Island
J4 Earl M. Hardy Box Canyon Sprs. Pres.
A1 Heyburn
F2 Lake Cascade
J6 Lake Walcott
F5 Land of Yankee Fork
I2 Lucky Peak
J4 Malad Gorge
A1 Mary Minerva McCroskey
F2 Ponderosa
J3 Three Island Crossing
C1 Winchester Lake

Counties

E2 Adams
I7 Bingham
G2 Boise
B3 Clearwater
G5 Custer
I3 Elmore
G2 Gem
I4 Gooding
D2 Idaho
H7 Jefferson
E5 Lemhi
C2 Lewis
K7 Power
A2 Shoshone
F3 Valley

Illinois

Towns

J8	Olney
F4, K8	Berry
J7	Bible Grove
K8	Bone Gap
J4	Boulder
F7	Bourbon
A1	Cameron
C2	Cuba
E3	Fancy Prairie
C4	Funks Grove
C3	Green Valley
D2	Havana
G8	Kansas
C2	Little America
I5	Loogootee
I1	New Delhi
I3	Panama
J3	Pocahontas
E3	Salisbury
A3	Speer
B2	Trivoli

Rivers & Creeks

J7	Big Muddy
K8	Bonpas Cr.
H5, K4	Kaskaskia
K7	Little Wabash
B5	Mackinaw
H1	Macoupin Cr.
C8	Mid. Fk. Vermilion
H8	N. Fk. Embarras
H2	Otter Cr.
D5	Salt Cr.
F4	Sangamon
J3	Shoal Cr.
A6	Vermilion

Points of Interest

F3	Lincoln Home N.H.S.
G7	Lincoln Log Cabin S.H.S.
E6	Railway Mus.
C2	Rockwell Mound
A6	Rte. 66 Mus.

Lakes

I4	Coffeen L.
J8	East Fork L.
B5	Evergreen L.
J3	Highland Silver L.
B5	Lake Bloomington
G8	L. Charleston
C2	L. Chautauqua
D5	L. Clinton
H4	L. Glenn Shoals
F2	L. Jacksonville
H3	L. Lou Yaeger
G7	L. Mattoon
H6	L. Sara
G6	Lake Shelbyville
F3	L. Springfield
E1	Mound L.
J7	Newton L.
G2	Otter L.
A2	Spoon L.
C3	Spring L.
D1	Stewart L.

State Parks & Rec

H2	Beaver Dam
D6	Clinton Lake S.R.A.
J4	Eldon Hazlet S.R.A.
G8	Fox Ridge
B3	Jubilee Coll.
C6	Moraine View S.R.A.
H5	Ramsey Lake S.R.A.
A3	Rock Island State Tr.
C2	Sand Ridge S.F.
F4	Sangchris Lake
J4	South Shore
J6	Stephen A. Forbes S.R.A.
F8	Walnut Pt.
B2	Wildlife Prairie
G6	Wolf Creek

Counties

G4	Christian
J6	Clay
G7	Coles
F7	Douglas
K8	Edwards
C1	Fulton
G1	Greene
I1	Jersey
D4	Logan
H2	Macoupin
C6	McLean
A3	Peoria
J8	Richland
F3	Sangamon
K2	St. Clair
C3	Tazewell
K7	Wayne
B4	Woodford

Indiana

Towns

D5	Bakers Corner
I7	Alert
H3	Cataract
J3	Cincinnati
E7	Eden
H7	Flat Rock
I5	Gnaw Bone
G4	Hall
C7	Leisure
G6	London
J1	Midland
H6	Nineveh
D6	Omega
B1	Pine Village
E3	Raccoon
C1	Rob Roy
H5	Samaria
A6	Wawpecong
A5	Young America

Rivers & Creeks

I4	Beanblossom Cr.
K8	Big Cr.
F7	Big Blue
G1	Big Raccoon Cr.
F3	Big Walnut Cr.
I6	Driftwood
I2	Eel
E6	Fall Cr.
K2	First
G8	Flatrock
H3	Mill Creek
K4	Salt Cr.
I8	Sand Cr.
D3	Sugar Cr.
A3	Wabash
D8, H4, J2	White
B4	Wildcat Cr.

Villes

J8	Butlerville
F3	Coatesville
C6	Curtisville
D8	Daleville
D4	Elizaville
G7	Gwynneville
D7	Huntsville
J3	Kirksville
G1	Knightsville
K5	Leesville
D6	Noblesville
I7	Petersville
J7	Queensville
E2	Russellville

B5	Russiaville
C5	Scircleville
J4	Smithville
H5	Spearsville
H6	Taylorsville

State Parks & Rec

I5	Brown County
J4	Fairfax S.R.A.
A6	Frances Slocum S.R.A.
E6	Ft. Harrison
J1	Greene-Sullivan S.F.
H2	Lieber S.R.A.
I3	McCormick's Creek
A6	Miami S.R.A.
H4	Morgan Monroe S.F.
D7	Mounds
J4	Paynetown S.R.A.
F2	Raccoon S.R.A.

Counties

A1	Benton
D4	Boone
H2	Clay
I8	Decatur
D1	Fountain
B7	Grant
J2	Greene
D6	Hamilton
E8	Henry
K7	Jennings
K4	Lawrence
E5	Marion
A6	Miami
I2	Owen
F1	Parke
F2	Putnam
H7	Shelby
C2	Tippecanoe

Iowa

Towns

C7 Waterloo
A8 Alpha
J8 Batavia
K3 Cambria
H2 Churchville
E1 Dana
H6 Evans
C5 Fern
G8 Holbrook
D2 Homer
F7 Irving
I2 New Virginia
I8 Ollie
K5 Plano
B2 Thor
F5 Van Cleve
B8 Westgate
H7 What Cheer
D6 Zaneta

Rivers & Creeks

C5 Beaver
D6 Black Hawk Cr.
A2 Boone
C3 Buck
A6, D8 Cedar
I5, K8 Des Moines
A1 E. Fk. Des Moines
K7 Fox
C3, F7 Iowa
H1 Middle
G7 N. English
H7 N. Skunk
G2 Raccoon
D3, F3, H6 S. Skunk
A5 Shell Rock
C8 Wapsipinicon
J3 White Breast Cr.
D6 Wolf Cr.

Lakes

G1 Bays Branch L.
B3 Big Wall Lake
A3 East Twin Lake
B3 Elm Lake
B2 Lake Cornelia
H4 Lake Red Rock
D3 Little Wall L.
B3 Morse L.
J5 Rathbun Lake
F5 Rock Creek L.
F3 Saylorville L.
A2 West Twin Lake

State Parks & Rec

B4 Beeds Lake
F2 Big Creek
C2 Bushy Creek St. Rec. Area
H5 Elk Rock
C7 George Wyth Mem.
E2 Holst S.F.
J5 Honey Creek
I3 Lake Ahquabi
I6 Lake Keomah
K6 Lake Wapello
E2 Ledges
K2 Nine Eagles
D5 Pine Lake
J4 Red Haw
F5 Rock Creek
K8 Shimek S.F.
J3 Stephens S.F.
E6 Union Grove

Counties

K5 Appanoose
B7 Bremer
B5 Butler
K3 Decatur
A8 Fayette
A5 Floyd
D4 Hardin
B1 Humboldt
G8 Iowa
F5 Jasper
H8 Keokuk
J3 Lucas
I2 Madison
H6 Mahaska
F3 Polk
E3 Story
K8 Van Buren
J7 Wapello
I3 Warren

Kansas

Towns

G7 Bazaar
K4 Corbin
D2 Denmark
D8 Dover
E3 Falun
H5 Furley
G4 Groveland
E3 Hedville
C5 Idana
J1 Lake City
G8 Lamont
B7 Lillis
A3 Lovewell
E5 Navarre
J3 Norwich
J8 Oak Valley
G8 Olpe
J5 Oxford
J1 Sawyer
B4 Talmo
D5 Upland
D1 Waldo
H2 Zenith

Lakes

H3 Cheney Res.
E7 Council Grove Lake
H6 El Dorado Lake
J8 Elk City Lake
I8 Fall River Lake
F3 Kanopolis Lake
A3 Lovewell Res.
F5 Marion Res.
C5 Milford Lake
I8 Toronto Lake
B6, B7 Tuttle Creek Res.
C2 Waconda Lake
D1 Wilson Lake

Rivers & Creeks

B6 Big Blue
K3 Bluff Creek
C5 Chapman Cr.
K4 Chikaskia
I8 Fall
J7 Grouse Cr.
G3 Little Arkansas
E6 Lyon
A5 Mill Cr.
F7 Neosho
D3 Saline
D3 Salt Creek
J2 Sand Cr.
E2 Smokey Hill
C8 Soldier Cr.

State Parks & Rec

I3 Cheney
I8 Cross Timbers
H6 El Dorado
I8 Fall River
C2 Glen Elder
E3 Kanopolis
D6 Milford
G3 Sand Hills
C6 Tuttle Creek
E1 Wilson

Points of Interest

D1 Garden of Eden
A1 Geographic Center of the Conterminous U.S.
B2 The World's Largest Ball of Sisal Twine

Counties

K1 Barber
F1 Barton
I8 Elk
E3 Ellsworth
D6 Geary
K3 Harper
G4 Harvey
A3 Jewell
F8 Lyon
A7 Marshall
C3 Mitchell
A8 Nemaha
H3 Reno
B4 Republic
D1 Russell
E3 Saline
I4 Sedgwick

Kentucky

Towns

B5 Berlin
G8 Bethany
H1 Black Gnat
K8 Black Snake
H4 Dog Walk
I2 Ella
H5 Gum Sulphur
G1 Holy Cross
E6 Judy
E8 Korea
J6 Lily
K1 Marrowbone
G3 Nevada
D4 Oxford
F7 Rosslyn
I4 Science Hill
G8 Shoulderblade
G2 St. Catharine
D7 Tilton
H7 Vincent

Rivers & Creeks

C5, K3 Beaver
H1 Big Pitman
D3 Cedar Cr.
J7 Collins Fk.
C2 Drennon
B4 Eagle Cr.
C7 Fleming
B4 Fork Lick
I7 Goose
I3 Green
E5 Houston Cr.
D3, F6, G4 Kentucky
C8 Kinniconick
J6 Laurel
C2 Little Kentucky
F6 Muddy
I8 Red Bird
G6 Red Lick
J7 Stinking
E6 Stoner Cr.

Villes

H6 Annville
H7 Booneville
K1 Burkesville
F1 Deatsville
C5 Connersville
K4 Coopersville
C7 Elizaville
E2 Finchville
B4 Gardnersville

J1 Gradyville
G4 Hyattsville
D3 Jacksonville
G5 Kirksville
D4 Minorsville
F3 Mortonsville
C5 Oddville
E7 Owingsville
D2 Pleasureville
B7 Plumville
G4 Preachersville
I2 Royville
I5 Shopville
E2 Southville
J4 Touristville
C3 Worthville

Lakes

E3 Beaver L.
B4 Bullock Pen L.
E8 Cave Run Lake
I2 Green River Lake
G3 Herrington L.
J3 Lake Cumberland
H5 Lake Linville
J5 Laurel River Lake
E2 Taylorsville L.
B4 Williamstown Lake
I6 Wood Creek L.

State Parks & Rec

A3 Big Bone Lick
C6 Blue Licks Battlefield S.R.P.
H8 Buckhorn Lake State Resort Park
J5 Cumberland Falls St. Resort Pk.
J4 General Burnside Island
K7 Kentucky Ridge
B5 Kincaid Lake
E4 Ky. Horse Pk.
I6 Levi Jackson Wilderness Road
F1 My Old Kentucky Home
F7 Natural Bridge State Resort Park
F3 Old Ft. Harrod
E2 Taylorsville Lake

Louisiana

Towns

I6 Pierre Part
D5 Aimwell
J8 Bayou Blue
H5 Catahoula
J2 Creole
B1 Dixie Inn
C5 Fort Necessity
H7 French Settlement
A5 Goodwill
A1 Ivan
A4 Log Cabin
B6 Monticello
C6 Newlight
J3 Pecan Island
D1 Pelican
G1 Singer
G2 Sugartown
G3 Turkey Creek
C4 Vixen
I7 Welcome

Lakes

I1 Black L.
G2 Bundick Lake
E4 Catahoula L.
D2 Clear L.
F3 Cocodrie L.
E3 Cotile L.
I3 Grand L.
C2 Kepler Cr. L.
B2 L. Bistineau
K8 L. Boudreaux
A2 L. Claiborne
E3 L. Iatt
I2 L. Misere
K7 L. Penchant
C6 L. St. Joseph
E5 Saline L.
I2 Sweet L.
D5 Turkey Cr. L.
F1 Vernon L.
J3 White L.

Rivers & Creeks

H5 Atchafalaya
G1 Bayou Anacoco
B3 Bayou D'Arbonne
C6 Bayou Macon
C1 Bayou Pierre
D1 Bayou San Patricio
E5 Black
C2 Black L. Bayou

C5 Boeuf
D4 Dugdemona
C4 Ouachita
F5 Red
C2 Saline Bayou
D6 Tensas
G2 Whisky Chitto Cr.

-Villes

I4 Abbeville
B2 Bienville
H5 Coteau Arnaudville
C5 Crowville
E4 Deville
E4 Fishville
A2 Haynesville
G2 Longville
D2 Marthaville
I6 Napoleonville
E4 Pineville
A3 Spearsville
C2 Springville
D4 Summerville
I4 Youngsville
E5 Wildsville

Parishes

H4 Acadia
G3 Allen
B2 Bienville
E5 Concordia
D1 De Soto
G6 E. Baton Rouge
G3 Evangeline
E3 Grant
I5 Iberia
D4 La Salle
C6 Madison
A5 Morehouse
G5 Pointe Coupee
E1 Sabine
J6 Terrebonne
A3 Union
I3 Vermilion
E2 Vernon
G6 W. Feliciana
D3 Winn

Maine

Towns

G1 Lynchville
E4 Athens
G5 Belfast
G4 China
I1 Denmark
G2 East Peru
K1 Lebanon
H3 Lisbon
E2 Madrid
F2 Mexico
D3 Moscow
I2 Naples
H2 Norway
H2 Poland
F3 Rome
H2 S. Paris
F3 Vienna

Towns Stars & Stripes

F4 Clinton
F5 Freedom
F8 Hancock
E4 Harmony
G5 Hope
F5 Jackson
H5 Jefferson
G5 Liberty
C7 Lincoln
E3 Madison
F6 Monroe
F5 Plymouth
H5 Union
F5 Unity
H5 Washington

Rivers & Creeks

C4 Big Wilson
B3 Brassua
D2 Carrabassett
A3 Dole
D1 Kennebago
C3 Kennebec
I1 Ossipee
D7 Passadumkeag
D6 Penobscot
A4 Pine
I2 Saco
F4 Sebasticook
D6 Sebec
G5 St. George
E8 Union
C5 W. Br. Pleasant

Villes

G6 Brooksville
C6 Brownville
F7 Cardville
F3 Chesterville
E4 Cornville
C4 Greenville
G6 Lincolnville
I5 Martinsville
H6 Oceanville
D5 Sangerville
A7 Stacyville
G5 Swanville
F4 Waterville

Lakes & Ponds

E8 Alligator L.
C2 Baker Pond
D8 Duck Lake
G3 Echo L.
E4 Great Moose L.
B4 Lobster Lake
I1 Moose Pd.
B4 Moosehead Lake
C4 Moxie Pond
E6 Pushaw
B5 Rainbow Lake
G4 Sheepscot Pond
F8 Spectacle Pond
F4 Unity Pnd.

Maryland

Towns
J7 Bishops Head
A5 Drybranch
A6 Forest Hill
G5 Friendship
D6 Gratitude
I6 Long Beach
G4 Mount Harmony
B1 Mount Pleasant
D8 Roberts
I3 Shiloh
E3 Silver Spring
E8 Starr
C7 Still Pond
D3 Sunshine
A2 Uniontown
I2 Welcome
C4 Woodstock

Rivers & Creeks
D7 Chester
F8 Choptank
A6 Deer
B3 N. Br. Patapsco
F4 Patuxent
G3 Piscataway
E1, J3 Potomac
B2 Sams
I8 Transquaking
E8 Tuckahoe Cr.
B6 Winters Run

Lakes
B8 Big Elk
B3 Liberty L.
A4 Prettyboy Res.
D2 Triadelphia Res.

State Parks & Rec
I6 Calvert Cliffs
G4 Cedarville S.F.
B8 Elk Neck
I5 Greenwell
B5 Gunpowder Falls
C6 Hart-Miller Island
F8 Martinak
G4 Merkle Wildlife Sanctuary
C3 Patapsco Valley
C2 Patuxent R.
K6 Point Lookout
A5 Rocks
F4 Rosaryville
D1 Seneca Creek

H2 Smallwood
J5 St. Mary's River
A6 Susquehanna

Villes
F5 Birdsville
D7 Burrisville
A6 Churchville
C3 Cooksville
D1 Dawsonville
B8 Earleville
D8 Ewingville
H4 Hughesville
B2 Johnsville
I4 Loveville
I4 Mechanicsville
A5 Shawsville
B3 Taylorsville
F7 Unionville
B1 Walkersville

Points
H5 Breezy Point
J4 Coltons Point
I6 Cove Point
I6 Drum Point
B8 Hack Point
K5 Piney Point
J4 Rock Point

Counties
B4 Baltimore
A3 Carroll
H3 Charles
H8 Dorchester
E8 Queen Anne's
F7 Talbot

Massachusetts

Towns
C5 Lincoln
A2 Ashby
D3 Berlin
E5 Dover
G6 Five Corners
A7 Georgetown
G8 Halifax
D1 Lambs Grove
I8 Long Plain
H7 Middleborough
C7 Nahant
F4 Nipmuck Pond
E8 Norwell
D4 Pine Rest
C1 Princeton
B6 Silver Lake
K7 South Westport
C3 Still River
F2 Sutton
E3 Upton

Lakes
C3 Bare Hill Pd.
F1 Buffumville L.
G7 Burrage Pd.
D3 Chauncy L.
D4 Fort Meadow Res.
B3 Hickory Hills L.
B4 Knops Pd.
B3 L. Shirley
A1 L. Wampanoag
E4 Lake Winthrop
I7 Long Pd.
A4 Mascuppic L.
F6 Massapoag Lake
A3 Massapoag Pond
F2 Singletary Pd.
E1 Stiles Res.
D4 Sudbury Res.
A1 Sunset L.

-Villes
G6 Barrowsville
G8 Bryantville
E4 Cordaville
F3 Fisherville
I6 Hortonville
H7 Lakeville
F4 Rockville
G4 Sheldonville
H8 Waterville
A1 Wellville

F3 Wheelockville
F3 Whitinsville

Counties
I7 Bristol
A7 Essex
A4 Middlesex
D6, E5 Norfolk
E6 Suffolk

State Parks & Rec
E4 Ashland
F6 Borderland
A7 Boxford
D4 Callahan
D4 Cochituate
K7 Demarest Lloyd
I6 Dighton Rock
B1 Dunn
J8 Fort Phoenix St. Res.
B5 Great Broo Farm
B6 Harold Parker S.F.
B2 Leominster S.F.
H7 Massasoit
A2 Pearl Hill
F2 Purgatory Chasm S.R.
D1 Rutland
E1 Spencer S.F.
C5 Waldon Pond S.R.
A7 Willowdale S.F.

Rivers & Creeks
F4, E5 Charles
I6 Cole
C5 Concord
B6 Ipswich
F4 Mill
B2 N. Nashua
A3 Nashua
H7 Nemasket
H5 Palmer
K7 Paskamanset
C2 Quinapoxet
F1 Quinebaug
A3 Squannacook
G6 Three Mile
B1 Whitman
G8 Winnetuxet

Michigan

Towns
I7 Hell
K8 Azalia
H6 Bell Oak
G4 Butternut
H3 Cascade
C8 Delano
G6 Easton
E1 Ferry
A2 Hannah
D6 Hope
I3 Lacey
D3 Paris
C1 Peacock
K7 Ridgeway
B7 Shady Shores
F8 Tuscola
H4 Westphalia

Rivers & Creeks
B7 Au Gres
E4 Chippewa
K1 Dowagiac
F3 Flat
F7, G8 Flint
G3, H4, J5 Grand
I3 Gun
C1 Little Manistee
H6 Looking Glass
A8, C2, E4, E6 Pine
D1 Pentwater
I2 Rabbit
B6 Rifle
K8 Saline
G6, H7 Shiawassee
I4 Thornapple
D5 Tobacco

Lakes
D1 Big Star L.
J6 Center L.
D3 Chippewa L.
B3 Crooked L.
F4 Crystal L.
K6 Devils L.
A2 Green Lake
I3 Gun L.
B5 Houghton L.
K3 Indian L.
H7 L. Fenton
B5 L. St. Helen
F3 Lincoln L.

A2, B7 Long L.
A3 Spider L.
C5 Wiggins L.

State Parks & Rec
D7 Bay City St. Rec. Area
I7 Brighton S.R.A.
K6 Cambridge Jct. Hist.
J3 Ft. Custer S.R.A.
I8 Highland S.R.A.
H8 Holly S.R.A.
A2 Interlochen
I8 Island Lake S.R.A.
J1 Kal-Haven Tr.
B6 Rifle River S.R.A.
G6 Sleepy Hollow
K7 Walter J. Hayes
B2 William Mitchell
I3 Yankee Springs S.R.A.

Counties
I2 Allegan
D6 Bay
I3 Barry
D4 Clare
C5 Gladwin
A4 Kalkaska
G4 Ionia
E4 Isabella
E3 Mecosta
B4 Missaukee
E1 Oceana
F6 Saginaw
J1 Van Buren
B2 Wexford

Minnesota

His Town
E8 Andree
D2 Brandon
D3 Carlos
J4 Evan
I5 Fernando
C6 Garrison
B7 Glen
E1 Herman
C4 Lincoln
F5 Marty
D3 Nelson
G7 Ramsey
H3 Raymond
J1 Russell
I4 Stewart
J1 Tyler
D1 Wendell

Her Town
F1 Alberta
C3 Bertha
H2 Clara City
D4 Clarissa
C1 Elizabeth
A6 Emily
J1 Florence
K1 Hadley
I7 Lydia
H1 Madison
J5 Nicollet
H4 Olivia
D3 Rose City
F8 Stacy
J2 Tracy
H7 Victoria
J3 Wanda

Rivers & Creeks
I3 Beaver
H4 Buffalo Cr.
F2 Chippewa
J2 Cottonwood
C5 Crow Wing
J4 Little Rock
D4 Long Prairie
I2, J6 Minnesota
C1 Otter Tail
B3 Redeye
E7 Rum
D4, F5 Sauk
G2 Shakopee

A3 Shell
E8 Snake
I1 Yellow Medicine
C3 Wing

Villes
G7 Albertville
E6 Brennyville
D4 Browerville
E5 Collegeville
D2 Evansville
F4 Georgeville
A4 Huntersville
K7 Janesville
I7 Lakeville
D2 Millerville
F4 Paynesville
H3 Renville
B2 Richville
J7 Shieldsville
D4 Swanville
K7 Waterville

Lakes
K7 Buffalo L.
G4 Eagle L.
C1 Fish Lake
A3 Fishhook L.
C4 Fish Trap L.
E8 Goose Lake
C5 Gull Lake
K5 Loon Lake
C2 North Turtle L.
C2 Otter Tail Lake
A1 Pelican Lake
B6 Rabbit Lake
D5 Skunk Lake
E3 Swan Lake
A2 Toad L.
A3 Wolf L.

Mississippi

Towns
E2 Leland
I2 Alcorn
E4 Black Hawk
E2 Bourbon
D5 Duck Hill
B4 Falcon
G5 Good Hope
I5 Hot Coffee
B6 Hurricane
K4 Kokomo
A5 Laws Hill
G7 Moscow
A7 Peoples
B4 Pope
C3 Rome
F2 Tallula
A8 Thrashers
D7 Whites
F3 Yazoo City

Rivers & Creeks
I3 Bayou Pierre
D3 Big Sunflower
J5 Bowie Cr.
H7 Buckatunna Cr.
C7 Chiwapa
G6 Chunky
B3 Coldwater
F2 Deer Cr.
K2 Homochitto
K7 Leaf
D6 Line Cr.
G5 Pearl
C6 Skuna
H5 Strong
A6 Tippah
C8 Tombigbee
I5 W. Tallahala
E3, G2 Yazoo
F5 Yockanookany

Lakes
C7 Aberdeen Lake
A4 Arkabutla L.
A8 Bay Springs L.
E7 Bluff L.
G2 Eagle Lake
B5 Enid Lake
A3 Flower L.
C5 Grenada L.
J6 Lake Bogue Homo
D2 Lake Bolivar
B3 Moon Lake
G7 Okatibbee Lake
A5 Sardis Lake

State Parks & Rec
D3 Florewood
C2 Great River Road
C5 Hugh White
A5 John W. Kyle
J1 Natchez
K3 Percy Quin
B7 Tombigbee
B7 Trace
A5 Wall Doxey

Villes
E7 Brooksville
G3 Brownsville
C5 Coffeeville
D3 Doddsville
A3 Evansville
G5 Forkville
H6 Garlandville
I4 Gatesville
A7 Geeville
I1 Hermanville
J1 Knoxville
K8 Leaksville
E6 Louisville
F2 Mayersville
B6 Springville
I5 Taylorsville
K1 Woodville

Counties
J1 Adams
I3 Copiah
J2 Franklin
K7 Greene
E4 Holmes
B8 Itawamba
H6 Jasper
G5 Leake
A5 Marshall
C6 Pontotoc
D3 Sunflower
C4 Tallahatchie

Missouri

Towns
B1 Plattsburg
F1 Amsterdam
H3 Bearcreek
C2 Camden
I6 Competition
K8 Couch
F2 Deepwater
K6 Dora
C8 Farmer
C5 Glasgow
B1 Grayson
F6 Henley
F8 Japan
A2 Kidder
H1 Milo
B2 Polo
B5 Prairie Hill
C7 Santa Fe
E8 Stony Hill
J3 Union City

Rivers & Creeks
K5 Beaver Cr.
D3 Blackwater
F8 Bourbeuse
C2 Crooked
K8 Eleven Point
F7, H6 Gasconade
B3 Grand
H2 Horse Cr.
J8 Jacks Fork
D4 Lamine
G4 Little Niangua
H8 Meramec
C4, E8 Missouri
A6 N. Fork Salt
F2 S. Grand
A7 S. Fabius
B8 Salt
J2 Spring

Lakes
F4 Lake of the Ozarks
A6 Long Branch L.
C7 Mark Twain L.
H4 Pomme de Terre L.
B4 Silver Lake
C1 Smithville L.
H2 Stockton Res.
B4 Swan Lake

State Parks & Rec
D4 Arrow Rock S.H.S.
H5 Bennett Spring

K1 Big Sugar Cr.
D6 Finger Lakes
D7 Graham Cave
G5 Ha Ha Tonka
F3 Harry S. Truman
D5, E4, E6, F2 Katy Trail
E3 Knob Noster
A5 Long Br.

Counties
K2 Barry
H2 Cedar
E6 Cole
D5 Cooper
I3 Dade
A2 Daviess
G4 Hickory
D1 Jackson
I1 Jasper
A7 Marion
F6 Osage
H7 Phelps
C2 Ray
K3 Stone
I7 Texas
G1 Vernon

Villes
K3 Abesville
K5 Bradleyville
C8 Curryville
B5 Darksville
F6 Etterville
A3 Farmersville
K6 Gainesville
I6 Hartville
H3 Humansville
E2 Kingsville
J3 Marionville
H1 Moundville
I1 Nashville
E4 Otterville
K1 Pineville
K7 Pottersville
G2 Rockville
J8 Summersville
K4 Taneyville
H5 Windyville

Montana

Towers

D3 Augusta
C4 Brady
F8 Buffalo
G6 Checkerboard
D1 Condon
G3 Elliston
B1 Essex
I4 Harrison
J1 Jackson
I7 McLeod
H7 Melville
F8 Moore
F2 Ovando
J6 Pine Creek
I4 Pony
D4 Sun River
I4 Willow Creek
I1 Wisdom

Rivers & Creeks

J3 Beaverhead
E6 Belt Cr.
B3 Birch Cr.
I1 Bitterroot
F2 Blackfoot
H4, I7 Boulder
A3 Cut Bank Cr.
E4 Dearborn
J2 Grasshopper Cr.
A2, A8 Milk
F2 Nevada Cr.
F8 Rossfork Cr.
K3 Ruby
A7 Sage Cr.
J8 Stillwater
D4 Sun
H7 Sweet Grass Cr.
I2 Wise

Lakes

D1 Big Salmon L.
G5 Canyon Ferry Lake
J4 Cataract Lake
J4 Ennis Lake
D3 Freezeout Lake
D7 Harwood Lake
A3 Hay Lake
F4 Holter Lake
J2 Lake Agnes
B5 Lake Elwell
B7 Lonesome Lake
I8 Lower Glaston Lake

A2 Lower St. Mary Lake
A3 Mission Lake
E1 Placid Lake
E1 Salmon Lake
C1 Swan Lake

State Parks & Rec

F7 Ackley Lake
H2 Anaconda Smoke Stack
K2 Bannack
G1 Beavertail Hill
F4 Black Sandy
H4 Elkhorn
D4 First Peoples Buffalo Jump
D5 Giant Springs
I8 Greycliff Prairie Dog Town
H2 Lost Cr.
I5 Missouri Headwaters
I4 Parker Homestead
F1 Placid Lake
F1 Salmon Lake
G4 Spring Meadow Lake
E4 Tower Rock

Counties

H5 Broadwater
E5 Cascade
C7 Chouteau
H2 Deer Lodge
C1 Flathead
A2 Glacier
G1 Granite
A6 Hill
H3 Jefferson
E3 Lewis and Clark
K4 Madison
F5 Meagher
J7 Park
C4 Pondera
I2 Silver Bow
J7 Sweet Grass
A4 Toole
G8 Wheatland

Nebraska

Towns

E5 Ericson
G4 Ashton
K2 Beaver City
J5 Blue Hill
J8 Bruning
A2 Burton
E1 Dunning
I8 Friend
F6 Fullerton
J1 Holbrook
B2 Long Pine
I7 Lushton
G2 Oconto
J2 Oxford
H4 Poole
K3 Republican City
E3 Sargent
F5 Scotia
E5 Spalding
H2 Sumner
G6 Worms

Villes

H2 Eddyville
G7 Hordville
E6 Raeville
G4 Rockville
I6 Saronville
F3 Westerville
K1 Wilsonville

State Parks & Rec

C4 Atkinson Lake S.R.A.
G4 Bowman Lake St. Rec. Area
E3 Calamus St. Rec. Area
H4 Cheyenne S.R.A.
I3 Fort Kearny St. Hist. Pk.
B7 Lewis & Clark S.R.A.
C1 Long Lake St. Rec. Area
C2 Long Pine St. Rec. Area
H5 Mormon I. S.R.A.
B6 Niobrara
G5 North Loup S.R.A.
A1 Smith Falls
F2 Victoria Springs St. Rec. Area
D7 Willow Creek St. Rec. Area

Lakes

E3 Calamus Reservoir
I2 Elwood Res.
I1 Johnson Res.
A7 Lewis & Clark Lake
C1 Moon Lake
F4 Sherman Reservoir

Rivers & Creeks

K1 Beaver Cr.
G8 Big Blue
D1 Calamus
E4 Cedar
J1 Medicine Cr.
F3 Middle Loup
A4 Niobrara
H1 Platte
C4 South Fork Elkhorn

Counties

C6 Antelope
E1 Blaine
E6 Boone
A5 Boyd
B1 Brown
H2 Dawson
J7 Fillmore
E4 Garfield
F5 Greeley
H5 Hall
H6 Hamilton
C4 Holt
B7 Knox
E2 Loup
I3 Phelps
C3 Rock
K8 Thayer
F4 Valley
D5 Wheeler